CONTENTS

TABLES

FOREWORD

Electoral participation is the touchstone of a healthy, responsive democracy. But how responsive is Britain's democratic process to its growing number of ethnic minority citizens?

Since the CRE first asked this question over twenty years ago, we have seen some encouraging signs. Yet there is still some way to go before British democracy can truly be called inclusive.

Serious and persistent doubts remain about ethnic minority engagement with the political process – and about the political system's engagement with ethnic minorities. As this report shows, despite increases in the proportion of ethnic minorities registered to vote, nearly a third of people from some ethnic minority groups did not actually use their vote in the 1997 election. And despite notable successes for ethnic minority candidates, ethnic minority representation in the political process is still unacceptably low.

Shamit Saggar's excellent report adds greatly to our understanding of the issue. Most previous studies have been based on stand-alone surveys of ethnic minority participation and voting behaviour. But this one makes a direct and extended comparison between ethnic minorities and the electorate as a whole. It enables us to judge how far we have travelled towards a fully inclusive democracy – and how far we still have to go.

All citizens, whatever their background, should have the right and the confidence to be involved and represented fully at all levels of the political system, as voters, candidates, activists, public appointees, councillors and Members of Parliament. This report presents a challenge to the political parties – and to us all – to go the extra distance, and make this ideal into a reality.

Sir Herman Ouseley
Chairman, Commission for Racial Equality

ACKNOWLEDGEMENTS

The research on which this report is based was carried out by the Committee for Research into Electoral and Social Trends, and jointly funded by the Economic and Social Research Council (grant number R000222123) and the Commission for Racial Equality. The Commission is grateful for the collaboration of the ESRC in supporting this pioneering study.

The origins of the project lie in several discussions between colleagues engaged in electoral research in the three years preceding the 1997 election. In particular, the author would like to acknowledge the input of Pippa Norris (Harvard), John Curtice (Strathclyde), David Sanders (Essex), Tony Messina (Tufts), and Andrew Geddes (Liverpool) in helping to develop the intellectual rationale and methodology for the booster project. In addition, the assistance provided by colleagues at Social and Community Planning Research (Lindsay Brook, Roger Jowell, Alison Park and Katarina Thomson) is warmly acknowledged. A special mention is reserved for Anthony Heath (Nuffield), who worked jointly with the author on early analysis of the data.

A related paper, 'Race: towards a multicultural electorate', co-authored with Anthony Heath, was presented to a special conference in May 1998 at Nuffield College, Oxford, on 'A Critical Election? Understanding the 1997 British General Election in Long-term Perspective'. This venue provided an important early opportunity to obtain academic feedback on the results of the project, and the author is grateful for the formal verbal comments of those who participated at the conference (especially the paper discussant, Richard Wyn Jones, Aberystwyth), as well as the informal responses of David Butler (Nuffield), Iain McLean (Nuffield) and Peter Kellner (*The Independent*).

In addition, written comments on an early draft were made by Colin Hann and Mayerlene Frow at the Commission and the author is grateful for these, as well as the former's more informal remarks on the race-politics scene.

Lastly, a small but significant vote of thanks goes to my wife, Rita Alfred, for her enduring patience with this and many other projects, as well as to our young daughters, Shelley and Shaan, who have done so much to fill the house with laughter (and chaos).

The rest, as they say in the research trade, is the author's effort and responsibility.

NOTE. *The views expressed in this report are those of the author and not necessarily those of the Commission for Racial Equality.*

PREFACE

Many who read this research report will think of it in the long tradition of reports on this topic published by the Commission for Racial Equality (CRE) and its predecessor, the Community Relations Commission (CRC). Indeed, it is almost a quarter of a century since the first of these appeared, based on a study of the autumn 1974 general election. Some of these reports have served as important, quasi-official records of ethnic minority electoral participation in British society, while others have appeared only as background research documents chiefly of interest to academic specialists. Together, these reports have made an important contribution to our understanding of the role of ethnic minorities in our country's democratic process. Of course, countless other research articles and volumes have appeared in the intervening years on this broad and fascinating topic (and one or two have featured the efforts of the author of this report). These research outputs have often complemented the CRC/CRE work, exploring in greater depth a number of basic questions about the relationship between ethnicity and political orientation and action. Their findings, incidentally, have also revealed some interesting insights into the often-complex relationship between mainstream democratic forms of political participation and other, non-conventional channels of political mobilisation and action. This particular report inevitably continues and extends that tradition, and, hopefully, will be received as an important additional stimulus to public policy discussion on political participation and ethnic pluralism. This debate is an important, though not especially well understood, part of public life in Britain in the late 1990s. If the report can help to fill that void, it will have been a worthwhile and effective exercise.

One of the principal aims of this project was to carry out a major piece of electoral research that went beyond a study of ethnic minority voting behaviour alone. In order to advance understanding of ethnic minority voting behaviour, the project set out to compare these voters with one another and also with their white counterparts. In this crucial sense, the study is a genuinely innovative and pioneering initiative. The chief purpose of this strategy was to promote insight into the extent to which ethnic minorities are integrated into the mainstream electoral process.

The key strategic advantage of this approach is that it allows direct and extensive comparison of ethnic minority political attitudes and electoral behaviour with those of the electorate as a whole. The comparative dimension is therefore the main point of differentiation between this project and earlier studies. By comparing across various minority communities as well as between minority and white citizens, the study is able to engage several key questions relating to political integration, democratic participation and social inclusion and exclusion. These questions cover not only the degree to which ethnic minorities are integrated into, or excluded from, the British electoral process but also the underlying factors explaining why some sections of the ethnic minority population fail to participate in the mainstream democratic process; and, using a range of empirical measures, they ask whether ethnic minorities are at least as committed to the electoral system as their white counterparts.

Furthermore, the study is able to address the question of how far, and in what sense, ethnicity is a fundamental political cleavage reflected in the attitudes and behaviour of ethnic minorities. For a long time, politicians, journalists, academics and other commentators have asked whether ethnic minorities are affected to the same degree by factors resulting in political differences among the (mostly white) electorate. Ethnicity appears to be an important line separating these two groups of voters, but it has been hard to judge whether this is a major, stand-alone divide or merely a reflection of socio-economic and circumstantial differences. This report throws fresh light on this old puzzle and presents the reader with a number of orthodox and unorthodox findings.

Behind this main research agenda lies a range of subsidiary issues that are also taken up in the report. The most pressing – and controversial – is the relationship between ethnic minority voters on one hand and the shaping of party strategy on the other. The report only addresses this important relationship indirectly, but the evidence clearly points to some powerful lessons for each of the major political parties. Second, the nature of political opinion among ethnic minorities and their white counterparts is an important area requiring further study. In particular, commentators have pondered over the role played by so-called racial issues in shaping both ethnic minority and white electoral behaviour. The report contains a number of pertinent findings on this question. Third, there is the perennial question (it seems) of the so-called 'race card' in British electoral politics. Controversy has raged on its influence in election campaigns, but there is little information on public attitudes to such campaign tactics. The report includes timely, and perhaps surprising, findings on this front. Finally, it is often superficially assumed that ethnic minorities are chiefly attached to a political agenda of their own, one that reflects not merely their socio-economic conditions and interests but also some kind of enduring racial or ethnic conditioning of political outlook and orientation. The evidence to back up this curiously widespread assumption has often been rather patchy, and a more systematic attempt to deal with it is also found in the report.

This report has been commissioned in order to extend radically existing understanding of ethnic minority political participation. It is linked to previous CRE work in this field and allows an important chain of continuity to be maintained. However, the overriding intellectual and practical interest of this venture lies in saying something of value about the political integration of Britain's 2.5 million black and Asian ethnic minorities. This central theme is backed up by a first rate comparative analytical framework which yields insights that go substantially farther than earlier work. As such, it is a pioneering step, brought about by an encouraging

CRE-ESRC collaboration, and is aimed at stimulating both specialist and popular opinion. If the report makes some inroads in that direction, the author will consider it an important job well begun.

Dr Shamit Saggar
London, April 1998

1. INTRODUCTION

There is a lot to be said for fresh, survey-based research aimed at advancing understanding of the political attitudes and electoral behaviour of Britain's ethnic minorities. Genuinely path-breaking research on these lines has generally been sporadic and patchy. Most of it has been conducted on the back of stand-alone surveys commissioned by the press and other interested groups, and, most worryingly, questions of comparison across white and ethnic minority groups have been relegated to the margins. Furthermore, little has been uncovered about the processes of political belief and opinion-formation underpinning voting choice, with the bulk of the existing data giving us little more than headline accounts of party loyalty. The aim of this report is to provide a useful insight into the nature and character of the ethnic minority electorate as compared with the white electorate. This comparative dimension is a new and long overdue addition to our understanding of race and politics in modern Britain.

Notwithstanding these criticisms of earlier research, it should be emphasised that it has undoubtedly contributed a great deal to existing understanding of the ethnic minority electorate among politicians, academics and others. It is now widely recognised, for example, that the sharply skewed voting loyalties among ethnic minorities have been relatively unaffected by social class, age and education. Whereas these 'conventional' sources of political difference may be said to have had an impact among white Britons, they appear to have had little, if any, real influence on their ethnic minority counterparts. If a similar picture becomes evident in the late 1990s – and the report will seek to shed light on this subject – this might suggest that cross-ethnic political integration remains as elusive as ever. Secondly, earlier studies have reinforced the point that the Left's *de facto* historic monopoly of minority electoral support has not gone unchallenged by the other major parties. Indeed, the last twenty years abound with examples of centre party and Conservative initiatives to appeal to minority voters. This report will seek to put such efforts in 1997 into context and to highlight those that can reliably be thought of as successes, however limited, for Labour's rivals. Finally, the earlier research has provided a useful service by pointing out that there may be serious problems of political abstention and alienation, albeit in pockets, among sections of the ethnic minority population. It has been difficult to assess the underlying scale and causal factors associated with minority non-participation, and one task for this report will be to focus on these patterns and to attempt to elucidate their probable causes and consequences.

The key strategic advantage of the research on which this report is based is that it allows direct and extensive comparison between ethnic minorities and the electorate as a whole, but it also serves other important purposes, principally to map the role of ethnicity in shaping ethnic minority political choice. It is commonplace in modern British politics to assume that the latter amounts to a function of the former. However, whether ethnicity trumps other, more familiar factors used to explain party choice is a question that depends on the degree to which they influence voting behaviour among voters at large. Secondly, it is clear that the bulk of party strategy on this front over the years has been founded on a belief in a common identity, and even a common cause, welding ethnic minorities together as a whole or as specific minority groups. This report examines the basis for this global approach and presents fresh evidence on its implications for future party strategy and 'ethnic campaigns'. Finally, there are important strands of opinion in Britain today on matters of race and ethnicity, and this report uncovers interesting patterns across a range of policies and propositions. In particular, evidence cited in the report suggests that, while there is some popular basis for playing the 'race card' during an election, this falls short of providing a compelling argument for pursuing such a strategy.

It should be added that electoral participation is only one, albeit fairly prominent, route to power and influence. Other legitimate and illegitimate options might include the politics of lobbying decision-makers (usually quiet and hidden from view) and the politics of protest and open conflict (sometimes involving riots and thus highly visible). This report does not purport to review these strategies in any detail, though it notes their occasional overlap with core, electoral-based strategies to gain political muscle. That said, it is perhaps erroneous to argue that these options are alternatives to the democratic electoral process as they often serve quite different functions. In short, electoral and non-electoral politics are usually conceptually different strategies for discrete groups seeking a political voice, and this report is under an obligation not to confuse their roles and degrees of effectiveness.

The unifying theme of the report's five main chapters is to evaluate the extent to which ethnic minorities are successfully integrated into the mainstream electoral process. Naturally, responses to this question start with measures of formal involvement (registration and turnout), but as the report notes, it is vital to proceed to further, supplementary measures. One of these is to examine the degree of variance in participation found among members of different ethnic minority groups. The evidence points to quite striking contrasts in some areas alongside strong patterns of commonality in others. Another measure is to evaluate differences between minority groups on one hand and their white counterparts on the other. Clearly, members of the former hold political views and adopt political behaviour that is substantially out of line with members of the latter, and the report narrows its gaze to the potential sources of such difference. It is these sources that have a real bearing on questions of political integration generally, and permit greater understanding of the internal heterogeneity in the political orientation of ethnic minorities.

It is also worth signalling at the outset that it can be all too easy to oversimplify the notion of political integration. For the purposes of this report, it is used to denote patterns of convergence and divergence in the political attitudes and electoral behaviour of different ethnic groups in Britain. The focus is primarily on black, Asian and white comparisons, although, where possible, attempts are made to establish any sub-group variance. Clearly, this is a rather broad-brush approach to political integration, since it reduces the concept to the level of inter-group similarities and dissimilarities that cannot be accounted for by surrounding environmental factors. The danger is that political integration measures might inadvertently mislead us into thinking that underlying sources of difference and tension are less significant. This worry can be particularly acute when observing the structure of political opinion and policy attitudes among various groups. Space does not permit an extensive discussion of the complex relationships between opinion and attitudes across a variety of issues and policy propositions. However, it is striking that many expected patterns in opinion and attitude often do not line up. Therefore, wider notions of what political integration signifies require some restraint, and this report is cautious about drawing too many or excessive generalisations. Inferences should be restricted to the narrow arena of electoral-based political participation and its attendant debates concerning democratic processes and institutions.

Political integration also depends on political representation. The penultimate chapter of this report is therefore devoted to an assessment of the performance of the 44 ethnic minority parliamentary candidates at the 1997 general election. With the number of such candidacies swelling to an all-time high, it is vital to be able to differentiate between genuine signs of progress in candidate selection and the froth of a large number of ethnic minority candidates in 'no-hope' seats. The evidence from 1997 contained elements of both, and also provided some unexpected insights into the effects of party label. This is revealing, not least because of the huge head of steam that has grown up in candidate selection contests over the presumed, though largely distorting, effects of ethnic origin. The 1997 election also included important breakthroughs. Most of these were related to the better-than-expected track record of senior ethnic minority incumbents, some of whom have proved themselves to be strong assets to party managers. Finally, the successful return in 1997 of one ethnic minority parliamentary candidate in a seat with hardly any ethnic minority voters indicates that an important mould has cracked, if not fully shattered, in debates about the representation of ethnic minorities as a political constituency. Attention is focused on this case to encourage debate as to whether it is a precursor of future trends.

The report comprises a further six chapters. Chapter two examines the question of electoral engagement and includes evidence on the basic forces driving inclusion or exclusion from electoral politics. Chapter three is concerned with voting choice, and in particular with the causes and consequences of the Labour Party's huge dominance over other parties. Chapter four considers the implications for party strategists, noting signs of good and bad news for all the main parties. Chapter five examines the structure of inter- and intra-group opinion on a range of issues, policies and philosophical propositions. Chapter six offers an assessment of candidate performance in 1997, and highlights the influence of 'ethnic campaigns' both in building and driving apart voting coalitions at local level. The report ends with a brief discussion of the relative importance of the 1997 general election for longer term prospects.

TERMINOLOGY

The term 'ethnic minority' is used in this report to denote people of South Asian, African and Caribbean origin. It is used interchangeably with the term 'minority'. Deployment of these terms as broad, umbrella labels is deliberate, in order to signify the wide variety of black and Asian ethnic groups resident in contemporary Britain. Where greater precision is required in the report with reference to specific component groups, departures from this convention are clearly signalled.

The reader's attention is drawn, in particular, to the report's delineation of the ethnic minority population into five principal categories: Indian, Pakistani, Bangladeshi, black-African and black-Caribbean, representing the largest and most recognisable minority groupings. A further, miscellaneous category was included, which allowed the analysis to include ethnic minority respondents who did not fall easily into, or perhaps even subtly distanced themselves from, the five-category scheme. The research did not extend to south-east Asian, ethnic Chinese and Indo-Chinese groups, although chapter six of the report, on parliamentary candidates, includes reference to these groups as candidates. Specific examination of these minority groups fell outside the scope of the original project, but is clearly an important area for further detailed study. The bulk of the commentary in the report relates to the large black and Asian categories, either as composite or disaggregated groups. Little direct reference is made in the report to the miscellaneous category because of the lack of agreed standardisation in its ethnic composition.

Inevitably, there is much debate on the subject of race and nomenclature, and this report may contribute some useful empirical insights to it. However, it should be stressed that, for the purposes of this report, no particular political or sociological inference should be drawn from the use of the above convention on terminology.

2. ELECTORAL INVOLVEMENT

The importance of electoral participation tends to be taken for granted in Britain today. In the case of ethnic minorities it is interesting that fairly close attention has been paid to questions of electoral engagement as part of a wider assessment of two processes. First, taking part in the electoral process and exerting political leverage through the democratic decision-making process, is often said to be a useful marker for involvement in mainstream society. Different degrees of mainstream electoral participation among different ethnic groups may therefore be understood as an indicator of wider integration. Formal political participation, like other forms of participation, can be measured on a fairly reliable scale. If groups shun participation in mainstream schooling, housing and other areas, we can surmise that electoral involvement is likely to follow a similar pattern. Usually such patterns line up, but where they do not, it is important to determine the scale of non-involvement and its underlying causes.

Second, full and robust ethnic minority participation in elections matters for the reputation of liberal democracy. For instance, democratic processes and institutions can be harmed in the longer run if large pockets of the would-be electorate remain aloof from participative norms. Moreover, if the disinterested groups can be easily identified, and if their non-participation cannot be easily explained in terms of social class or other factors, it is important to explore the underlying reasons for such collective abstention. One obvious worry is that democratic institutions, such as mainstream political parties, are at fault. At the very least this may be the consequence of parties' poor track record, collectively, in appealing to minorities, and at worst the inevitable result of previous hostility towards not just minority interests but the very question of minority citizenship and voting rights.[1] Parties and politicians, in other words, cannot make unfettered claims about the quality of the democratic system unless this is adequately reflected in participation patterns across all ethnic groups.

POPULATION AND CITIZENSHIP

Before detailed assessments can be made about the reputation of democratic institutions, however, it is necessary to introduce some basic qualifications. The first is to isolate the degree to which legal citizenship defines other rights, including voting rights. We should be clear that, historically, the United Kingdom has tended to grant voting rights on rather more generous terms than many countries across continental Europe and, indeed, elsewhere. Most post-war immigration from the New Commonwealth was usually associated with the enjoyment of full political rights by the immigrant newcomers. The vast majority of them held some form of recognised British nationality, while those who did not frequently normalised their nationality status within a short period of time. The upshot of this legacy has been that we can examine the electoral participation of black and Asian ethnic minority groups without having first to consider whether they are likely to enjoy political rights or not. This point may be a live and vexed question in countries such as Germany and Italy, but it is largely irrelevant in the British context.[2]

Citizenship and voting rights are, of course, only of relevance if contested or the subject of political division themselves. In large measure, Britain has been exempt from this kind of controversy, although elements of the far right continue to question the legitimacy of the political-legal settlement surrounding large scale non-white immigration in the 1950s and 1960s. The proportionate size and geographic spread of the minority population, therefore, dominate the picture in Britain. Table 1 gives a breakdown of the population of the UK at the 1991 Census, and clearly highlights the 2:1 ratio of Asians to black Africans and black Caribbeans within the ethnic minority population. The table also shows clearly that, at 5.5 per cent, non-white ethnic minorities account for a very moderate slice of the total population. Non-black or Asian minorities comprise around a fifth of all ethnic minorities and cannot be easily overlooked. (They are largely picked up in a miscellaneous analytical category in the survey boost, as the report's aims are geared principally to surveying black and Asian groups.) It should also be stressed that these figures, based on the 1991 Census, are likely to have been out of date by the time of the 1997 general election. One commentator has suggested that a further 12 per cent growth in the overall ethnic minority population might have taken place between 1991-96, and perhaps as much as a 20 per cent growth projected over the period 1991-2001.[3]

Table 1. Ethnic origins of UK resident population, 1991

Ethnic group	No. (000s)	% of total population	% of non-white population
All	54,889	100.0	
white	51,874	94.5	–
Non-white	3,015	5.5	100.0
black Caribbean	500	0.9	16.6
black African	212	0.4	7.0
black other	178	0.3	5.9
black total	*890*	*1.6*	*29.5*
Indian	840	1.5	27.9
Pakistani	477	0.9	15.8
Bangladeshi	163	0.3	5.4
South Asian total	*1,480*	*2.7*	*49.1*
Chinese	157	0.3	5.2
Other Asian	198	0.4	6.6
Other non-Asian	290	0.5	9.6

Source: 1991 General Census

Table 2 sketches a picture of the geographic distribution of whites and ethnic minorities collectively, using official Census data. The obvious messages in this table are hard to miss. First, minorities are overwhelmingly concentrated in urban parts of the country, with their attendant constituency characteristics and political histories. Second, London and the south east swallow up well over half of the entire ethnic minority population compared with less than a third of whites. Third, despite several concentrated pockets of minority settlement in northern industrial towns and cities, there is no particular tendency among minorities to be over-concentrated in those regions, whereas the opposite is true of the West Midlands. Finally, with over three-quarters of minorities clustered in the south east and the Midlands, it is fairly clear that party strategies aimed at attracting minority support will need to be similarly geographically focused.

Table 2. Regional distribution of UK resident population, by ethnic origin, 1991

	Total %	white %	Ethnic minority %
Britain	100.0	100.0	100.0
England & Wales	90.9	90.5	97.9
England	85.7	85.1	96.5
North	5.5	5.8	1.3
Yorkshire	8.8	8.9	7.1
East Midlands	7.2	7.3	6.2
East Anglia	3.7	3.8	1.4
South east	31.4	29.9	56.2
(Greater London	12.2	10.3	44.6)
South west	8.4	8.8	2.1
West Midlands	9.4	9.1	14.1
North west	11.4	11.6	8.1
All metropolitan districts	*42.0*	*39.9*	*78.0*
All non-metropolitan districts	*58.0*	*60.1*	*22.0*
Wales	5.2	5.4	1.4
Scotland	9.1	9.5	2.1

Source: 1991 General Census

The rates of British citizenship among different ethnic groups vary widely, as Table 3 shows. Black Africans exhibit the highest level of non-British citizenship. This group tends to comprise large numbers of students, graduate trainees and other essentially temporary residents among whom it would be unusual to see large numbers relinquishing the citizenship of their country of origin. Where actual immigration has been involved (as opposed to temporary residency), it might be expected that higher rates of British citizenship would follow. Indians, Pakistanis and black Caribbeans have rather similar levels of British citizenship (around 9 in 10); all three groups have their origins in labour migration (and political refuge) dating from the 1950s to the 1970s. It is the Bangladeshi group that stands out: barely three-quarters claim to be British citizens, a fact that reflects their more recent immigration history, as well as a naturalisation logjam. Finally, there are some interesting variations in dual citizenship. This appears to be a genuine option for all minority groups, except Indians. Apart from Indian government rules restricting dual citizenship, this may also be due to this

Table 3. Citizenship, by ethnic group, 1997

ARE YOU A BRITISH CITIZEN?

	white %	Indian %	Pakist %	Bangla %	Bl-Af %	Bl-Car %	Misc %
Yes, British citizen	97.4	85.9	81.3	73.9	49.0	89.1	83.1
No, citizen of another country	2.0	13.2	13.8	17.4	43.0	6.1	14.5
Both countries	0.6	0.9	4.9	8.7	8.0	4.8	2.4
Total %	100.0	100.0	100.0	100.0	100.0	100.0	100.0
Total No. [3327]	[2601]	[227]	[123]	[46]	[100]	[147]	[83]

Source: BES 1997, merged file

group's much earlier immigrant history, with the result that many Indians today are relatively distant from their (or their Indian parents') national origins. Equally, rapidly falling rates of dual citizenship may be associated with higher economic standing and educational attainment, areas where this group has led other minorities in recent years.[4] In fact, according to these data there is not a great deal to distinguish Indians with dual citizenship from their white counterparts.

REGISTRATION

In order to play any part in a general election individuals need to be registered to vote. Access to the electoral roll is possible through the annually-updated Electoral Register, although its reliability tends to be undermined by the effects of high levels of residential mobility, shared occupancy, and difficulties in comprehending a bureaucratic form, as well as varying degrees of interest in public affairs. Registers are notoriously out of date at any given election, clogged up with surprisingly large numbers of people who are either no longer alive or who have moved away.[5] Certain parts of the country, especially many inner city constituencies, are characterised by unusually high household turnover, leading to even further deterioration in the registration picture. Moreover, poor registration rates among minorities have been linked to voter disinterest and disillusionment.[6] Little can be done in the short term to tackle the deeper roots of such alienation, although it may be possible for pressure groups and other campaigns to sweep significant numbers of abstainers onto the register. Operation Black Vote (OBV), which is discussed in more detail in chapter four, is one group whose work in the 1997 election campaign stands out. The organisation's central aim was to encourage minority voters to register to vote, thereby equipping literally new voters – though not necessarily young voters – with the basic tools for democratic involvement. In the long run, it is unlikely that parties will be able

Table 4. Electoral registration, by ethnic group, 1997

IS YOUR NAME ON THE ELECTORAL REGISTER?

	white %	Indian %	Pakist %	Bangla %	Bl-Af %	Bl-Car %	Misc %
Yes, at this address	91.8	93.8	88.6	89.1	78.2	87.8	86.7
Yes, at another address	4.8	3.1	1.6	2.2	5.9	8.2	4.8
Yes, at this address and another	0.0	0.0	0.0	0.0	0.0	0.0	0.0
Yes, don't know address	0.3	0.0	0.0	0.0	3.0	0.0	0.0
Yes (all categories)	*96.9*	*96.9*	*90.2*	*91.3*	*87.1*	*96.0*	*91.5*
No	2.8	2.6	9.8	6.5	11.9	3.4	4.8
Don't know	0.2	0.4	0.0	2.2	1.0	0.7	3.6
Total %	100.0	100.0	100.0	100.0	100.0	100.0	100.0
Total No. [3328]	[2601]	[227]	[123]	[46]	[101]	[147]	[83]

Source: BES 1997, merged file

to overlook such efforts if they can be shown to raise registration levels, over and beyond the increased participation and awareness produced by single, high interest elections.

Earlier studies of ethnic minority voting patterns have suggested that minority registration rates are lower than the rate for whites.[7] The data in Table 4 broadly confirm this picture in 1997, although respondents were in fact being asked to recall accurately registration details that would have been over two months out of date by the time of the survey. All the Asian groups exhibit rates at or about that of their white counterparts, with none of them falling appreciably below the nine in ten prevailing level. Indians, once again, lead the minority cohort with a rate that in fact outstrips that for whites. Similar figures have been found in earlier local studies, suggesting that these rates are credible.[8] Black rates among both component groups were lower, though it was the rate among black Africans that was dramatically out of line with the rates among most ethnic minority groups. However, once account was taken of black registration at other addresses (than where the respondent was interviewed), rates improved quite considerably and, indeed, black Caribbean registration rivalled the very high rates seen among whites and Indians. This suggests that pre-election claims of significant levels of under-registration among black Caribbeans were probably fairly wide of the mark.[9]

TURNOUT

The picture sketched thus far is one of reasonably high levels of engagement, with pockets of largely predictable over- and under-commitment. The acid test, of course, lies in casting a vote on polling day itself. Unless registered groups turn out in sufficient numbers, much of the earlier effort to get them to pursue political affairs in stakeholder terms will come to little. Potential voters are subject to a number of short and long term influences in shaping their turnout rates. At the short term end, it is often claimed that personal circumstances, household and family commitments, and even the state of the weather are likely to have an impact. This is true, but only to a degree, since looking at likely turnout in these terms can mask groups of voters who, despite being registered to vote, were never really likely to cast their ballots. These 'voters' can be regarded as hardcore abstainers (that is, they show no real interest in an election or its outcome) or as serial abstainers (they have rarely, if ever, voted, and lack of interest in politics is only one of several underlying factors). For political parties, the focus tends to be on trying to reach those at the margin who are somewhat doubtful or diffident about going out to vote. The hardcore or serial abstainers, in contrast, seem like monumental challenges, especially in resource terms, although, of course, if there are enough of them, parties and others will be forced to address some of the deeper causes of their inactivity.

Table 5 shows turnout rates across the different ethnic groups at the 1997 general election. A familiar pattern emerges, with high electoral involvement among Indians again reflected in a turnout rate higher than that for whites, and by a margin that was far from negligible. The rest of the picture is equally predictable. There is little to distinguish between the Pakistani and Bangladeshi turnout rates: both were reasonably high and not significantly out of line with the rate for whites. It was a slightly different story among both black Africans and black Caribbeans. In both cases, turnout rates dipped far below those of all other ethnic groups, suggesting, at the very least, that there was a serious problem of mobilisation. These low rates are certainly similar to those found in some earlier studies. It is worth recalling that a sense of looming black political alienation underpinned a number of debates about minority politics in the run-up to the 1997 election[10] expressing concern about

Table 5. Turnout, by ethnic group, 1997

DID YOU MANAGE TO VOTE AT THE GENERAL ELECTION?

	white %	Indian %	Pakist %	Bangla %	Bl-Af %	Bl-Car %	Misc %
Yes	78.7	82.4	75.6	73.9	64.4	68.7	65.1
No	21.2	17.6	24.4	26.1	35.6	30.6	34.9
Don't know	0.0	0.0	0.0	0.0	0.0	0.7	0.0
Total %	100.0	100.0	100.0	100.0	100.0	100.0	100.0
Total No. [3328]	[2601]	[227]	[123]	[46]	[101]	[147]	[83]

Source: BES 1997, merged file

27

black abstention, though, curiously, on the basis of polling data which showed an even lower possible black turnout. Ironically, some might conclude that the figures for blacks in Table 5 actually reveal a higher turnout level than had been feared before the election.

Either way, it is hard to deny that the figures present a serious issue for democratic participation. If the factors driving significantly lower black turnout rates are other than circumstantial – that is, they cannot be explained by geography (lower turnout is associated with inner urban constituencies) or social class (generally higher among middle class than working class groups) – then it is likely that some fairly specific racial considerations are at play. Such considerations might reasonably include black political alienation based on racial exclusion and distancing from mainstream society. Systematic patterns of discrimination bound up with repetitive tendencies towards repressive self-identity cannot be ruled out as powerful processes linked with such racially defined indicators of political involvement. This is an important issue for democratic participation, facing not just these communities but also democratic institutions such as political parties and elected government more generally.

The position of Indians is worthy of some special comment. At election after election, studies have shown that they have higher levels of registration and turnout than any other minority group, and even, on occasion, their white counterparts. Setting aside narrow debates about the underlying reasons for this pattern, it is fairly clear that a large – indeed the largest – segment of the ethnic minority population contains citizens with considerable commitment to, and presumably faith in, the mainstream electoral process. This must surely amount to a powerful template, perhaps even a model, for those politicians who wish to emphasise the representative and responsive nature of British democratic traditions.

OVERVIEW

Taken together, these figures indicate that there are identifiable variations in the degree to which different ethnic groups are engaged in the democratic electoral process. However, two caveats apply. First, the variance from one group to another tends to follow a fairly predictable path, the significance of which is difficult to assess conclusively. That is, ethnic Indians are often associated with higher overall involvement than other minority groups, but it is not clear whether this is mainly a reflection of underlying socio-economic differences. Second, the magnitude of some of the inter-group differences is perhaps less than might be thought or predicted. Certainly, some groups' propensity to register and turn out regularly stands below that of others, but in the main the picture found among many of the minority groups is quite clustered. Most minorities share a lot in common with most other minorities in their electoral involvement, contrasting at the margin with their white counterparts. However, no group falls dramatically short of the underlying minority participation rate, though some occasionally remain above it. Arguments and debates concerning substantial democratic underparticipation among minorities must therefore take care to evaluate these variations accordingly.

3. VOTING CHOICE

The voting patterns of ethnic minorities are an important feature of the political landscape in Britain for four inter-related reasons. First, party allegiances can, and often do, make a material difference to the politics of delivering racially explicit and targeted public policy. Labour-supporting minorities might therefore argue that their endorsement implies that the party is under a special obligation to show itself to be responsive to policy demands and expectations from the minority communities. Whether party managers and leaders are willing to accept such responsiveness remains a moot point, however.[11] Second, measuring party loyalties has the potential for telling us how far traditional ideological and other differences between the parties are reflected in minority voter preferences. Equally, are patterns of strong Labour voting accounted for in terms of traditional, non-racial forms of party differentiation, or is this structural advantage to be explained in terms of inter-party differences on matters of race and ethnicity? Third, changes in party choice, even over long periods of time, are significant because of what these movements, where they exist, tell us about underlying developments in the socio-economic circumstances and policy preferences of different ethnic groups. Finally, it may not be possible to explain sharp disparities between the voting patterns of white voters and those of ethnic minorities in circumstantial terms alone (that is, in terms of class or geographical differences). In this case, minority voting patterns are at least partly driven by factors related to a common ethnicity, and the task is to highlight as precisely as possible the dynamics of ethnically-related forms of political belief and action.

HISTORICAL CONTEXT

A great deal has been said and written about the political allegiances of Britain's ethnic minorities.[12] Historically, it is no secret that British ethnic minority voters have backed the Labour Party in staggering numbers, and repeatedly. As Table 6 shows, in most elections it has been typical for four in five minority voters to support Labour. Of course, much of this earlier evidence is based on stand-alone surveys of minorities, but they nevertheless provide a reasonably reliable indicator of sharply skewed voting allegiances. These figures summarise the distribution of the overall minority vote, freezing out of the picture any signs of sub-group variations.

The two-fold picture portrayed in the table is unmistakable: that is, in all elections for which there are usable data (1974-97), the overwhelming bias to Labour among ethnic minority voters is self-evidently out of line with the varying fortunes of Labour among white voters. It should be remembered that the period up to 1997 included only one Labour general election triumph and in fact spanned a long era of national electoral strength for the Conservatives. Labour's strong lead among minority voters over this period stands in fairly sharp contrast to its poor track record in attracting non-minority voters. Second, the Labour bias appears to be relatively insulated from short-term electoral trends. For instance, the national collapse in electoral support suffered by the party in 1983 is not reflected in any degree among minority voters. Minorities remained loyal to Labour in an extremely cold climate. Equally, the gradual rise in Labour's fortunes thereafter – up to and including the 1997 election – is poorly reflected in minority support patterns. In other words, the Labour Party is probably enjoying saturation levels of minority electoral support, and has been doing so for over a generation. Non-Labour voting has consistently been both poor and flat. Tory support has historically remained locked at the one in ten level, and even the so-called breakthrough in 1987 turned out to be a false dawn.

Table 6. Labour and Conservative support among ethnic minorities at the general elections in 1974, 1979, 1983, 1987 and 1992

	1974* %	1979 %	1983** %	1987 %	1992** %
Labour	81	86	83	72	81
Conservative	9	8	7	18	10

* October 1974 general election
** Recalculated weighted average of Asian and Afro-Caribbean support levels

Sources: Adapted from: Community Relations Commission, *Participation of Ethnic Minorities in the General Election of October 1974*, London: CRC, 1975; Commission for Racial Equality, *Votes and Policies*, London: CRE, 1980; Commission for Racial Equality, *Ethnic Minorities and the 1983 General Election*, London: CRE, 1984; Harris Research Centre, 'Political attitudes among ethnic minorities', unpublished data set JN98746 London: Harris, 1987; A. Ali & G. Percival, *Race and Representation: ethnic minorities and the 1992 elections*, London: CRE, 1993.

The backdrop against which the 1997 findings are to be assessed is clear-cut, and involves three questions. First, did Labour's considerable national revival yield a premium among minority voters? Second, how is the minority, non-Labour vote – and specifically the minority Tory vote – to be interpreted? Third, what insights can be obtained from examining inter-minority group variations in relation to the underlying distribution of the white vote?

BACKGROUND TO THE 1997 CAMPAIGN

In the light of Labour's dominance among ethnic minority voters, interest has historically lain in the question of the likelihood of any real Tory or third party breakthrough. Indeed, with Conservative strategists actively trying to court minority voters since the 1970s, there has been little that is very new in the waging of so-called 'ethnic campaigns'.[13] The Tories, in fact, have very little to show for their efforts going back over half a dozen elections. Therefore, it came as no real surprise when the 'ethnic campaign' began in earnest some four months before the spring 1997 election.[14]

The focal points for commentators were essentially twofold. First, what, if any, prospects were there for a genuine Conservative breakthrough, however patchy and limited? This interest was stoked mainly by the growing realisation that, as polling day neared, the 1997 general election was increasingly likely to be a poor year for the Tories. In these circumstances, a breakthrough among any group within the electorate would have been a considerable achievement in itself. The suggestion that ethnic minority voters might prove to be suitable territory for a Tory revival was astonishing, and at the limits of plausibility. Second, if Labour's *de facto* monopoly was to be reinforced, perhaps even extended, in 1997, what evidence was there that Labour allegiances had remained unaffected by pockets of growing prosperity and upward social mobility experienced by some sections of the minority electorate? In other words, so strong had Labour support among minorities become during the 1980s and 1990s that, it was suggested, it amounted to an instinctive habit. The Labour Party might then be not so much a first choice as a natural choice, the roots of which probably went deeper than the pull of election campaigns. If this was the case, the prospects for Tory (and indeed Liberal Democrat) electoral strategy appeared gloomier than ever.

Going back to the Conservative record, it does not seem unreasonable to suggest that this aroused considerable despair among the party's backroom strategists, for three principal reasons. First, the idea of wooing minority voters was anything but new in 1997 and, indeed, the party could cite, rather frustratingly, a twenty-year effort on this front, for the first time in 1976, and most recently in 1986 with the establishment of the high profile Conservative One Nation Forum. Second, the most plausible moment for a sustained advance had probably passed by the mid 1990s. The 1997 election ended the Conservatives' long spell of electoral dominance and, with it, their best opportunity to attract new groups to the party cause. Finally, the task of tackling latent anti-immigrant sentiment at grassroots level in the party had probably come and gone in the early 1990s with John Major's initial, though unsustained, attempts to sketch a vision of an inclusive, tolerant society. The rising tide of anti-European Union feeling both at grassroots and elite levels in the party thereafter was sometimes mistakenly linked to residual anti-foreigner attitude.

VOTING IN 1997

The evidence suggests that the 1997 election reinforced earlier patterns of ethnic minority voting when measured in aggregate. Breakthroughs for the Tories or others *cannot* be claimed from the evidence. Saturation levels of Labour voting had been achieved in earlier elections and, as expected, were replicated in the 1997 contest. The figures in Table 7 tell the story: weighted summaries of Asian and black voters as well as non-white voters as a whole demonstrate clearly an old and familiar pattern of Labour dominance. It is clear that the four-in-five 'iron law' of previous elections came into operation once again, with fewer than one in ten minority voters backing the Conservatives in 1997.

This was a poor performance for the Tories on two grounds. First, some pre-election polling data from MORI had suggested that their standing was somewhat higher.[15] Indeed, Tory support among Asians a month before polling day was estimated to be as high as 25 per cent by MORI, a figure which only served to put party strategists onto a false trail. Second, in previous elections Tory non-white support had successfully breached the 10 per cent mark and the natural expectation was that a further modest improvement might have been achievable. In the event it was not, and minority support for the Tories slumped (from an already low base), as it did among the electorate at large.

However, Table 7 also shows a clear contrast between Asian and black voters. While Labour voting among Asians was very high and entirely in line with the four-in-five benchmark, it touched nine in ten among black voters. In addition, while the rate of Tory voting among Asians remained extremely low, it was more than double the rate among black voters.

Electoral support for the Liberal Democrats was pitifully low, remarkably even among Asians and blacks. Whatever the hall-marks of Liberal Democrat positions on race and immigration issues over the years, it would seem that few among the minority electorate chose to reward the party and its predecessors at the election. Arguably, this amounts to a fairly clear defeat for propo-nents of the view that ethnic minority electoral choice is based on a party's policies on certain issues.

The only ray of light for the Liberal Democrats came from Bangladeshis, the ethnic minority group among whom the party's support stood highest (and by quite a large margin; see Table 8). This is significant, since the party is especially strong and well-organised on the ground in inner East London, having established a long tradition of doorstep, community politics. This area, of course, is the hub of Bangladeshi population concentrations, both in London and in the country as a whole.

Table 7. Distribution of Asian and black votes, 1997

	Asian %	black %	Total %
Conservative	10.8	4.2	8.5
Labour	80.6	89.2	83.5
Liberal Democrat	3.5	3.0	3.3
Other	1.3	0.0	0.8
Refused/don't know	3.8	3.6	3.7
Total %	100.0	100.0	100.0
Total No.	[314]	[166]	[480]

Source: BES 1997, merged file

INTER-GROUP COMPARISONS

It is both possible and desirable to draw further distinctions in the character of ethnic minority party choice. Furthermore, it is important to introduce some comparison with white voters in 1997. Table 8 gives details, revealing several important variations. Most importantly, it shows that the appeal of Labour's rivals rises and falls considerably from one ethnic minority group to another. For instance, Tory voting was desperately scarce across all minority groups, except Indians, who were two, three and even four times more likely to vote for the Tories than other Asian and black groups. To be sure, at 14.4 per cent in 1997, their rate stood at around half the rate found in a Tory-weary white electorate. Arguably, in an otherwise generally dismal picture, here is some sign, however limited, of Tory progress among what remains the largest single minority group.

Table 8. Distribution of votes, by ethnic group, 1997

	white %	Indian %	Pakist %	Bangla %	Bl-Af %	Bl-Car %	Misc %
Conservative	30.4	14.4	6.5	2.9	4.6	4.0	14.8
Labour	45.7	81.8	79.6	76.5	87.7	90.1	70.4
Liberal Democrat	17.8	2.1	4.3	8.8	4.6	2.0	9.3
Other	3.8	0.0	4.3	0.0	0.0	0.0	3.8
Refused/don't know	2.2	1.6	5.5	11.8	3.1	4.0	1.9
Total %	100.0	100.0	100.0	100.0	100.0	100.0	100.0
Total No. [2582]	[2048]	[187]	[93]	[34]	[65]	[101]	[54]

Source: BES 1997, merged file

Considerable variance is also seen in the Liberal Democrats' support. Pakistanis and, to a lesser degree, Bangladeshis and black Africans view support for the Liberal Democrats as a viable alternative to Labour in a way not shared by Indians (who veer rather more to the Conservatives as an alternative) and black Caribbeans (who are a remarkably one party oriented group). Finally, the data reveal that fourth and/or fringe party support simply does not exist among minority voters, with the singular exception of Pakistanis. In 1997, these fourth and/or fringe options usually included support for local, single issue, minority candidates and parties, the Referendum Party, and other minor causes. Such comparable support outside the three-party mould is only found among white voters (mainly involving the Referendum Party or the Green Party), and even then to a slightly lesser degree.

The data record a picture of resounding Labour success and stark Tory and Liberal Democrat failure. It is very difficult, however much one tries, to put any gloss on non-Labour performance, other than to say that 1997 was at least no worse than some earlier elections. These conclusions are based on the distribution of the minority vote. A radically different – and possibly more incisive – approach would be to examine the ethnic distribution of the votes gathered by the parties.

ETHNIC SOURCES OF PARTY SUPPORT

Table 9, which looks at the sources of all the votes gained by the parties from ethnic minorities in 1997, reveals a potentially significant pattern at work. The numerically much larger Asian electorate tends to dwarf its black counterpart in terms of the reliance placed by all the major parties on Asian voters. That is, although some parties get many more minority supporters than others, all parties get the lion's share of their minority support from Asian sources. This is due, chiefly, to demographic size, demographic characteristics, and differential registration and turnout. Across the minority electorate at large, there are two Asian voters for every one black voter.

At party-specific level, the bias can be even greater. For instance, the Tories picked up the overwhelming majority of all their minority support from Asian voters. In party strategy terms, this means that the small number of ethnic minority Tory voters are almost invariably Asian. This is the product of two factors: the greater size of the Asian electorate, and the greater popularity of the Tories among Asians relative to blacks (11 versus 4 per cent). In the case of Labour, too, reliance is biased towards Asian voters, though rather less dramatically than in the case of the Tories, and a similar picture emerges in the case of the Liberal Democrats – two in three minority Labour-voters and Liberal Democrat-voters are Asians. The upshot of this finding is that, while 'ethnic campaign' strategies are usually couched in general, ethnic minority terms, the reality is that all the parties are in fact either holding on to and/or competing for Asian voters. Such reliance also has its drawbacks. One danger is that increasingly focused campaign messages might risk edging out interest in, and the interests of, black minority voters.

Table 9. Ethnic minority group source of parties' votes, 1997

	Conservative %	Labour %	Lib Dem %	Other %	Refused/dk %	Total % share of minority vote %
Asian	82.9	63.1	68.8	100.0	82.4	65.4
black	17.1	36.9	31.3	0.0	17.6	34.6
Total %	100.0	100.0	100.0	100.0	100.0	100.0
Total No.	[41]	[401]	[16]	[4]	[17]	[480]

Source: BES 1997, merged file

Another is that very heavy reliance on Asian voters (as seen in the Conservative profile) might risk the party's being viewed in no-go terms by black voters. Finally, the more even splits in Labour and Liberal Democrat sources of support (in line with the approximate sizes of the Asian and black electorates) might mask a tendency towards gradual Asian-voter depletion. This possibility would mean that Labour was becoming increasingly reliant on black voters at the level of voter recruitment and retention, but that this pattern was hidden by the far greater number of Asian voters.

OVERVIEW

The evidence from the distribution of votes in 1997 shows that there was little that was new in minority voting patterns. A bold line of continuity ran through them in 1997 and in earlier years. Labour further consolidated its virtual monopoly of the allegiances of this section of the electorate. The Tories, meanwhile, took some comfort from fairly buoyant levels of support from Indians, the largest minority group; however, these levels only compare well against the nadir reached in national levels of Tory support. Ultimately, the biggest influence on party strategies may not be the distribution of minority votes but the proportionately larger influence of the Asian electorate compared with other minority groups. In essence, small changes in a party's rating among Asian voters will yield comparatively large movements across the minority electorate as a whole. In addition, the tight geographic clustering of Asians means that parties may conclude that, on rational, vote-maximising grounds, they have somewhat more to gain from wooing this group of voters than others. It is probably unlikely in the short term that this factor will lead to an eclipsing of the interests of other minorities – in campaigning terms at least – but the possibility cannot be ruled out in the longer term. A lot will depend on the approach and tactics of activists within the parties themselves, not least during periods of structural and organisational renewal, as witnessed in the Conservative Party since mid 1997.[16]

4. PARTY STRATEGIES

The strategic thinking behind political parties' campaigns towards ethnic minority voters has been the subject of extended comment over the years. This has been precipitated partly by the staggering lead enjoyed by Labour over its rivals and partly by the lack of results for Tory and centre party efforts over the years. An added factor has been the widespread belief that economic and social embourgeoisement among selected minority groups would lead to a decisive break-up of Labour's stranglehold. The Jewish parallel has been cited on countless occasions to show the potential for rightward drift.[17] Labour's commanding position, it has been suggested, would be weakened by factors that were both beyond its control as well as in its historic nature to promote. The source of a major dilemma for party strategy is therefore clearly apparent.

IMPLICATIONS OF 1997 VOTING PATTERNS

How should the evidence presented in chapter three be interpreted? Broadly speaking, three principal conclusions can be drawn. First, while ethnic minority support for parties other than Labour is very low, there are some definite, though isolated, glimmers of hope for the Conservatives. For instance, as previously noted, in an electoral year that proved to be very bad for the Tories among white and minority voters alike, just under 15 per cent of Indians voted for them in 1997. This is significant, partly because of the numerical leverage that this proportion yields in the single largest minority group, and also because it is so considerably out of line with other minorities. Again, it is important to know whether this support reflects the socio-economic status of Indians or is, in

40

fact, genuine evidence of a rapport, even trust, that has grown up between this group and the party. In any case, it is vital to bear in mind the dismal electoral context within which Indian Tory voting reached this high level.[18]

Second, the huge Labour lead in 1997 seems to have been earned without much evidence of active Labour campaigning to attract minority support. Such 'ethnic campaigning' as there was in 1997 was chiefly a Tory affair, with some signs of Liberal Democrat activism. Labour's success, therefore, was achieved without any significant campaigning effort and was largely assured months, or even years, before the election itself. Indeed, there appear to have been very few, if any, noticeable ethnic or racial dimensions to this commanding lead. This, in turn, might lead us to speculate that a strong Labour bias is at work across several generations of minority voters. Its foundations are partly historical and partly ideological, and have served to build a virtually impenetrable fortress around Labour's treasure.[19] The interesting question would be to see how far this characterisation is true of younger minority voters. Notably, a MORI pre-election survey found that some 19 per cent of Asian respondents described their political views as 'more Conservative than their parents',[20] tacit evidence that the Conservatives are in fact under-polling among this group of voters.

Third, Labour's lead in 1997 amounted to a testimony to its determination to hold on to minority voters, while restricting policy pledges targeted exclusively at them. Critics have claimed that this was driven by the fear of establishing too close a relationship with minorities and thus risking an electoral backlash, and that the party chose a low profile approach accordingly. In any case, its appeal was largely couched in non-race specific terms, and it succeeded. The Tories' pitch, meanwhile, rested almost entirely on the colourful recital of a cultural, values-based argument, suggesting that there was a natural affinity between so-called Asian values and Conservative values. Its slogan virtually amounted to: 'Your values are our values; our values are your values'. This claim arguably succeeded in flattering several groups of minority voters, but without influencing them. Therefore, the obvious conclusion would seem to be that Tory strategy might learn from Labour in avoiding direct, ethnic-based appeals. Indirect appeals and 'mainstreaming' minority concerns within party platforms appear to be the most credible route forward.

ETHNIC MINORITY PERCEPTIONS

Labour's strategic strength among ethnic minorities in 1997 is enviable. It would be hard to think of another social group whose voting loyalties are so overwhelmingly skewed to the benefit of a single party. Over the years it has been conventional to explain this bias in terms of push and pull factors, the former referring to various anti-Tory biases, while the latter includes positive bonds between Labour and its minority constituency. However, running through these perspectives are questions about how the major parties are perceived by the minority communities. Such perceptions are founded on three important building blocks. First, there are evaluations of the parties in terms of their position and track record on so-called minority or race issues. This report is not the place to rehearse what, precisely, is meant by the notion of a race issue.[21] However, there is an *a priori* assumption in British politics that minorities will pay close attention to policy and practice in fields such as anti-discrimination law, racial violence, employment-based equal opportunities and immigration. Second, minority voters can be expected to follow, and hold views on, the full range of mainstream political issues that make up any given election campaign. In recent years these will tend to have been issues such as health, education, law and order, unemployment, and so on. Parties are able to recognise that minority voters arguably share much of this mainstream agenda with white voters and, on this basis, build campaigns that accentuate this overlap. Again, the question must be why, on mainstream issues, is Labour able to trounce its opposition in securing minority support? Third, it is of course quite likely that minority voters assess party reputations through some combination of racial and mainstream issues; that is to say they may see a potential racial twist or dimension in otherwise mainstream issues. For instance, education as an issue is principally viewed as being about schools, class sizes, the national curriculum, attainment standards, and so on. However, while recognising this picture, minorities may also be sensitive to questions such as school exclusion policies, hidden discrimination in the curriculum, minority under-achievement, and so on. The issue is therefore both racial and mainstream at one and the same time.

'MINORITY ISSUES' AND QUESTIONS OF 'TRUST'

The reputation of a political party is the product of many years of activity – and inactivity – on policy and presentational style. Table 10 shows how the Asian electorate views the parties on so-called Asian interests. The data are revealing on two key grounds. First, it is clear that the proportion who said they trusted the Tories most (15 per cent) was smaller than the proportion who declared an intention to vote Conservative in this particular survey (a surprisingly high 25 per cent). The implication is that the Tories are the beneficiaries of other issues and concerns. Second, there is clear evidence of a continuing anti-Tory mood among Asian voters on so-called Asian interests alone. No single party elicited more than a 9 per cent score on the question of which party was trusted least; the Tories, however, were caught at the short end of no less than a third of the Asian electorate, evidence enough of a strained relationship.

Put together, this suggests that future Tory campaigning would be wise to avoid overemphasising the party's credentials on Asian interests. The party's reputation is low; non-ethnic factors make as much or more contribution to its support; and where its reputation does count, it is probably as a negative, vote-losing influence.

Table 10. Trust and Asian interests, 1997

WHICH PARTY DO YOU TRUST MOST [LEAST] TO LOOK AFTER THE INTERESTS OF ASIAN PEOPLE IN THIS COUNTRY?

	Most %	Least %
Conservative	15	32
Labour	51	9
Liberal Democrat	2	9
Other	1	9
None of them	21	21
Don't know	14	23

Source: MORI, 1997

In terms of party strategy, the lesson seems to be that the Conservatives have relied too heavily on arguments and approaches that are poorly suited to their task. The 1997 MORI survey also shows clear evidence of stronger Asian bullishness before the election on issues such as the economy.[22] The upshot was that by plugging away at their economic management record, the Conservatives in 1997 played to a genuine lead among Asian voters on the issue itself. The trouble was that party strategists did not recognise the party's limited strengths when this was most needed.

PARTY AND POLICY PREFERENCES

Turning to mainstream issues, the evidence from 1997 demonstrates that, on the basis of policies traditionally and ideologically associated with each political party, Labour was clearly the favoured party among minority voters. Table 11 shows that the party stood head and shoulders above the Conservatives on a major, bread-and-butter election issue. A cursory glance at the figures in the table suggests that there is an interesting contrast in the opinion structures of Asians and blacks. For example, it is clear that, relative to Asian voters, black voters overwhelmingly endorse an explicit raise-tax-and-spend option. With such an opinion profile, an 'ethnic-minorities-as-disproportionate-winners' electoral strategy makes a good deal of sense when directed towards minorities across the board. In the case of Asian voters it seems to make less sense, although it is nevertheless probably fairly well guided. It is worth adding that there may be some group-specific factors at work leading, albeit rather indirectly, to some of the differences shown in these data. More sophisticated research is needed to assess the likelihood and degree of such group effects, as well as some attempt to theorise ethnically-related political attitudes and behaviour.

Table 11. Policy preferences: tax-and-spend strategies, 1997

SUPPORT FOR DIFFERENT TAX-AND-SPEND OPTIONS

	white	Indian	Pakist	Bangla	Bl/Af	Bl/Car	Misc
	%	%	%	%	%	%	%
Reduce taxes and spend less on health	2.3	11.5	11.4	4.3	3.0	6.8	6.0
Keep taxes and spending unchanged	24.8	30.8	22.8	30.4	24.8	19.7	25.0
Increase taxes and spend more on health	69.0	52.0	56.9	56.5	68.3	66.7	59.0
None of these options	2.7	2.6	2.4	2.2	2.0	3.4	7.2
Don't know/not answered	1.1	3.1	6.5	6.5	2.0	1.4	1.2
Total %	100.0	100.0	100.0	100.0	100.0	100.0	100.0
Total No. [3328]	[2601]	[227]	[123]	[46]	[101]	[147]	[83]

Source: BES 1997, merged file

The Indian and Pakistani groups contain sizeable numbers who favour traditional, right-wing, tax-and-spend positions. Interestingly, support for this proposition barely registered at all among white respondents. Another feature of the data is that minority support for traditional left wing positions, while strong, was muted in comparison with the backing expressed by whites. Some seven in ten whites embraced a 'state interventionist' stance, while minorities included large proportions who preferred to sit on the fence. The essential point here is that there are sharp variations in support for specific options across different ethnic groups. The preference among Asians for options that are not overtly identified with the Labour Party is telling, and suggests that these may affect the way they vote.

FUTURE PROSPECTS

The short term picture of ethnic minority party preferences and voting loyalty is fairly clear cut. A variety of demographic, historical and ideological factors combine to produce what seems like a position of unassailable dominance for the Labour Party. However, parties are not the only players involved in shaping the political orientations of minority voters. Minority pressure groups and various self-help bodies play a role, too. In addition, the trajectory of a party's strategy in the past may not be a reliable guide to its future strategy. Some interesting hints in this respect can be gleaned from the 1997 election and its aftermath.

First, the 1997 election was the first one where a national, single issue pressure group campaigned to boost minority participation. Operation Black Vote, a dedicated campaign established by Charter 88 and the 1990 Trust, managed to achieve considerable exposure in the period up to the election. It differed from earlier efforts to raise minority political awareness, first because it was genuinely non-partisan (whereas many earlier initiatives were not) and, second, because its preoccupation was with electoral registration and turnout. That said, it prosecuted the argument in support of minority electoral leverage on the basis of an old and familiar theme, namely that of 'ethnic marginals', as an inducement to parties to address OBV's core agenda. In other words, it sought to make electoral geography work for minority voting interests by identifying a list of marginal seats in which minority voters held strategic influence. There was nothing new in this claim, which was first deployed in a Community Relations Commission report on the autumn 1974 election.[23] Moreover, others such as Zee TV, an independent Asian satellite station, sought to make similar political capital in 1997.[24] It is very difficult to measure the real impact of OBV in terms of its 'ethnic marginals' strategy, not least because the secret ballot serves as a barrier to knowing whether a differential white/minority swing at constituency level was the principal reason that seats changed hands in 1997. Overall, it is much more likely that the forces of a pro-Labour swing across the board superseded any specific ethnic minority effect. That said, OBV could claim some credit in ensuring that ethnic minority affairs (at a very general level) were not entirely buried from view in an otherwise non-racial election campaign.[25] Since May 1997, OBV has declared its intention to carry on its promotional and educational work. It seems likely that its influence will pick up momentum in the run-up to the next election, not to mention the impending elections for the European Parliament. Meanwhile, it has wisely focused its attention on questions of electoral reform and on developments within party structures aimed at attracting minority involvement.

Thus, the black and Asian electorates were the subjects of unprecedented efforts to mobilise their electoral force. In 1997 this objective was singled out by OBV, and to a lesser degree by an initiative known as 'Race for the Vote' (a loose cross-group campaign body). The combined impact of both was such that the threat of presumed black non-participation featured as a central and continuing element in all media coverage of race matters. The dilemma for OBV and others was that, in highlighting black abstention, they unintentionally raised the possibility that black electoral muscle was, in truth, rather less potent than had been claimed.

Second, the political landscape after 1997 is one in which the long term rebuilding of Conservative organisational structures has emerged as one of the most pressing concerns for the Opposition. Of course, a lot can and has been claimed about the need for a more diverse, mass party membership, and the symbolic significance of ethnic minority representatives. It is impossible to tell how far such initiatives in the Conservative Party will go in the longer run. However, it is clear that the post-1997 context amounts to a rare occasion in which the party not only finds itself out of office but also severely diminished in morale and organisational capacity. In this respect the situation resembles the mid 1970s when the Conservatives first began a root-and-branch assessment of their appeal to ethnic minority voters and established specific projects to tackle deficiencies. A new-look Tory party may be a long way off, but the underlying question of its basic attractiveness to different sections of the electorate amounts to a legitimate and far-reaching issue.[26] It is this factor, above all else, which is most likely to drive substantive reforms, change the internal culture of the party, and project a fresh and credible image to potential minority recruits.

Third, the geographic concentration of ethnic minorities in certain seats and parts of the country means that their voting strength is potentially greater than if they were evenly dispersed. Hypothetically, therefore, electoral and ethnic geography can be combined to wield political muscle. In many marginal seats in 1997 a great deal of attention was paid to trying to get minority voters to act as an ethnic voting bloc, and, indeed, OBV and others published various target constituency lists to this end. However, on the debit side, it should be remembered that such an impact requires differential swings among white and ethnic minority voters in very marginal seats and, moreover, that such swings need to be attributable to 'ethnic' rather than 'mainstream' factors for there to be a real chance of tipping the balance in a genuine 'ethnic marginal'. In 1997 such a strong impact was probably only seen in two seats (Bethnal Green and Bow, and Bradford West). In both cases strong Labour majorities were decimated by Asian Tory candidates who succeeded in splitting the local ethnic minority vote. This may not have been the outcome that proponents of the 'ethnic marginals' campaign intended, but these cases undoubtedly reveal the underlying potential of marshalling ethnic blocs. It is this implied threat – or promise – that serves to concentrate the minds of party strategists keen to uncover fresh and powerful approaches to electoral competition.

5. ISSUES AND POLICIES

It has long been assumed that ethnic minorities vote in elections on the basis of two related factors: first, in terms shaped by so-called ethnic issues related to being ethnically distinct in British society (discrimination, equality, exclusion, etc); and second, on the basis of a common ethnic identity or solidarity. In this section we examine the evidence to support, or detract from, such an assumption. It is clear that the evidence partly supports such a claim – albeit at a very generalised level – but it is far from conclusive. The implications of such an assumption are widespread, since this will affect the way political parties pitch their campaigns to attract, or hold on to, minority voters. It matters, too, because of the knock-on effects on political organisation and mobilisation within the minority communities themselves. Finally, it should not be forgotten that ethnic minority voters have an obvious stake in so-called mainstream issues, such as jobs, education, housing and law and order, although it is debatable whether their expectations are identical to those of white voters.

RACIAL AND ETHNIC VOTING

It is customary for politicians in Britain to think of ethnic minorities as being characterised by a special, though not open-ended, interest in racial and ethnic affairs. What this means is that political concerns are seen as being either closer to or farther from the interests of black and Asian people. In terms of actual issues, one frequently hears reference being made to so-called ethnic or racial issues. For instance, for many years, the whole question of immigration policy has been accepted as a staple item on the ethnic minority agenda. This was because it was easy to see how public discussions over immigration were in fact about policies and procedures that mainly targeted black and Asian immigration. Black people and Asians, as a result of their recent direct immigration experience, therefore, were bound to have a lot at stake and be concerned about immigration policy as a political issue, according to this viewpoint. As large scale primary immigration declined, attention among black and Asian people tended to switch to policies governing secondary immigration involving family reunification. However, as immigration as a whole has fallen, especially from South Asian and Caribbean sources, so too has the salience of the issue. Political analysts have been quick to pick up on this sea change as it affects white voters while curiously missing out on its obvious impact on ethnic minority voters. Elsewhere, the same perspective resulted in the claim that ethnic minorities were more interested than whites in policies governing race relations, anti-discrimination and the promotion of stable racial integration. The race relations laws, to be sure, became overtly identified with the stuff of racial issues and racial politics and, by association, with ethnic minorities themselves.

This association was perhaps understandable, given the underlying focus of these laws on improving conditions and opportunities for ethnic minorities who were – and remain – the subjects of discrimination and exclusion. But it was understandable only to a degree. This is because it is easy to overlook the possibility that policy questions such as immigration control and combating racial discrimination might be concerns shared by white voters. Indeed, these issues may conceivably be of greater concern to white voters than to their black and Asian counterparts. To be sure, twenty to thirty years ago, the kernel of the immigration issue in British politics was defined as addressing, perhaps appeasing, white fears and suspicions over the influx of newcomers from the New Commonwealth. To that extent it was a white issue, since it was only debated by politicians in terms of its saliency for, and impact on, white voters. Likewise, it is important to remember that the idea of maintaining and monitoring effective laws to curb racial

in the interpretation of the question. Some respondents, quite reasonably, might have taken the question to be an assessment of immigration in terms of its success or failure for the minority communities themselves, or perhaps even for individuals specifically. Aware that there are higher concentrations of black Caribbeans among lower socio-economic groups, it is hardly surprising if the sceptics have used this question as a proxy indicator or reflection of their own broader socio-economic status. Other groups within the survey are likely to have either taken the question to be a metaphor for their own experiences or else interpreted it more broadly as an opportunity to comment on the value, or otherwise, of immigration to society generally. Either way, strikingly different results were found which cannot avoid comment, and some serious concern.

POSITIVE DISCRIMINATION

Not surprisingly, there were some very significant patterns in the data obtained on the thorny topic of positive discrimination. As Table 13 makes abundantly clear, not only is there virtually no support for the notion of positive discrimination among white voters, there is also precious little backing to be found from black and Asian sources. That said, the global picture contains some interesting variations. Indians and black Caribbeans come closest to the overwhelming rejection seen among whites. The other minority groups – Pakistanis, Bangladeshis and black Africans – all profess a modicum of support, though plainly nothing like the levels that might be required to make such a policy a realistic possibility. Once more, we should not forget that some of these variations might be the result of socio-economic differences among members of different minority groups.

The picture painted in this table appears to be fairly decisive, but this is based on a reading of its findings at one level only. The problem stems from the term 'positive discrimination' which, in several

Table 13. Views on positive discrimination, by ethnic group, 1997

RACIAL PRIORITY VERSUS COMPETITION

	white %	Indian %	Pakist %	Bangla %	Bl/Af %	Bl/Car %	Misc %
Black people and Asians should get priority	1.9	7.0	18.7	13.0	16.0	6.8	3.6
Black people and Asians should compete for jobs	97.0	89.0	74.8	84.8	81.0	90.4	95.2
Don't know	1.1	4.0	6.5	2.2	3.0	2.7	1.2
Total %	100.0	100.0	100.0	100.0	100.0	100.0	100.0
Total No.[3326]	[2601]	[227]	[123]	[46]	[100]	[146]	[83]

Source: BES 1997, merged file

policy-making and political circles, has been seen in a slightly pejorative way. It is no secret that for many years British public life has tended to view the entire concept of positive discrimination with suspicion, as being reminiscent of a form of alien and unfair logic in public affairs. For much of this time this doctrine has been closely linked to US-style affirmative action programmes, with much of the damaging publicity that has usually gone with such an association and few of the benefits. With this in mind, it is perhaps not surprising to learn that both white and minority opinion reflect this wider context, with few voters, of whatever ethnic background, prepared to endorse such an obviously tainted policy.

EQUAL OPPORTUNITIES

With this evidence in mind, it would be interesting to see what levels of support there are for other related propositions, especially those geared toward providing ethnic minorities with specific, time-delineated opportunities in fields such as employment training and vocational education. We might speculate that support might be somewhat greater precisely because of the removal of a blanket approach and a counter-productive label. If this is the case, it demonstrates a subtle yet powerful distinction in public opinion.

The evidence contained in Table 14 helps to unpack this suggestion a little. Three central observations appear to stand out and are worthy of mention. First, it is striking to see how far the group of white voters who feel that equal opportunities have gone either much too far or too far proportionately dwarfs any signs of comparable opinion among blacks and Asians.

Table 14. Views on equal opportunities for ethnic minorities, 1997

EQUAL OPPORTUNITIES FOR ETHNIC MINORITIES HAVE:

	white %	Indian %	Pakist %	Bangla %	Bl/Af %	Bl/Car %	Misc %
gone much too far	5.6	2.2	0.0	2.2	0.0	0.0	2.4
gone too far	21.4	2.6	2.4	4.3	1.0	0.0	7.2
about right	42.8	41.9	30.9	45.7	30.3	21.1	32.5
not gone far enough	23.8	43.6	44.7	41.3	45.5	66.7	47.0
not gone nearly far enough	2.7	5.7	16.3	2.2	19.2	10.9	8.4
don't know	3.7	4.0	5.7	4.3	4.0	1.4	2.4
Total %	100.0	100.0	100.0	100.0	100.0	100.0	100.0
Total No [3323]	[2598]	[227]	[123]	[46]	[99]	[147]	[83]

Source: BES 1997, merged file

Nearly a third of whites take this tough, critical position compared with very small numbers of ethnic minorities, suggesting signs of a clear division. However, it should not be overlooked that the question might elicit sentiment not just on the degree of equal opportunities in public policy but also on the pace of change. Second, there appear to be strong elements of support for the status quo option across all groups, though, significantly, Indian and Bangladeshi opinion lines up most closely with that of whites. Again, socio-economic factors may drive this variance, but the opinion structure of the Bangladeshi group then looks puzzling, to say the least. Third, there appear to be strong cross-black and Asian coalitions of support for the idea that reforms could go further. This contrasts with the much smaller proportion of whites who share this position. In fact, twice as many ethnic minorities as whites believed equal opportunities had not gone far enough, while more than three in four black Caribbeans, in particular, took a similar or even more sceptical view.

The major caveat worth reporting is that one in four whites backed the view that such opportunities were underdeveloped and/or under-implemented. This finding is important because it shows that political efforts to build and expand equal opportunities are not as susceptible to unqualified white disapproval – or veto – as is sometimes imagined. Although, as Table 13 showed, barely 2 per cent of whites gave their support to positive discrimination in employment, too few even to mention some might say, their response was significantly more liberal when the question of promoting the life chances of ethnic minorities was put in policy terms. The key distinction appears to be one of rights versus opportunities. Positive discrimination as a political label, intellectual concept and rhetorical doctrine might well have been politically undermined precisely because it feeds an impression of unfettered and one-sided granting of entitlements on the basis of ethnic group membership alone. It is thus perceived in a zero-sum context and, unsurprisingly, condemned in similar terms. Meanwhile, the concept of equal opportunities, while far from universally supported by white opinion, is at least contextualised in a more constructive manner. Its logic is principally geared toward removing unwarranted and illegitimate barriers (that is, discrimination) to ethnic minorities denied legitimate opportunities to compete in labour and other markets. In this regard, it is a proposition that can at least appeal to progressive, liberal sentiment among whites (as well as minorities). It may also have some attraction for politicians who feel obliged to promote a meritocratic vision of not only job opportunities but also social mobility and social inclusion more generally.

INTEGRATION

Underlying views on specific policies lies public sentiment on the more abstract subject of the policy and experience of integration in Britain. Social researchers have regularly surveyed this topic, and it is useful to see the shape of public opinion as revealed through electoral analysis. Table 15 paints this picture, revealing some decisive, and perhaps surprising, findings.

Table 15. Views on ethnic integration, by ethnic group, 1997

IT IS BETTER:

	white %	Indian %	Pakist %	Bangla %	Bl/Af %	Bl/Car %	Misc %
to keep customs and traditions	21.4	36.3	43.1	58.7	34.7	26.9	31.3
to adapt and blend	73.0	53.5	52.8	32.6	59.2	66.2	57.8
don't know	5.6	10.2	4.1	8.7	6.1	6.9	10.8
Total %	100.0	100.0	100.0	100.0	100.0	100.0	100.0
Total No. [3318]	[2597]	[226]	[123]	[46]	[98]	[145]	[83]

Source: BES 1997, merged file

To start with, the level of support for the 'staying apart' option is high across all groups, though more than twice as popular among whites as Bangladeshis. Most noteworthy is the fact that, some two generations after Britain began its momentous transition into a multicultural, multi-racial society, as many as three-quarters of all whites reject this position. With the passage of time, the vast majority of them have adopted a 'mixing together' stance. However, this is also the case among the minority communities, though to a rather smaller degree. Oddly, those minority groups who back such an approach to integration conform to no obvious pattern. Substantially higher levels of support for 'mixing' among Indians and blacks, compared with, say, Bangladeshis, defy any pattern we might expect to see on the basis of socio-economic status, educational attainment or length of residence. Black Caribbeans exhibit the highest rate of support for 'mixing', again indicating that this type of question might be interpreted in terms of retrospective assessments of settlement styles, patterns and experiences as opposed to prospective predictions of integration trajectories.

Questions about integration are sometimes deployed for what they tell us about groups' overall evaluations of the various strategies that frame race relations. A note of caution should be introduced, however. This is because assessments of integration can often be a measure of several different things, some of them related and some not. For instance, over many years researchers have been fond of focusing on inter-ethnic rates of marriage or partnership. For fairly obvious reasons, this was often seen as a reliable proxy for views on both integration and the practice of integration. But the question of integration may also be of relevance in the workplace (that is, the idea of black and Asian people as co-workers, colleagues, subordinates or bosses), in social relations (as friends, acquaintances, etc), and in housing (as neighbours or in terms of 'ethnic neighbourhoods'). In fact, there are many areas where integration sentiment can be measured, and it is certainly possible that different patterns of opinion might be found from one to another. Any respondent – white, black or Asian – may be expected to view the prospect of a casual workplace friendship with someone from another ethnic group somewhat differently from the idea of a new, in-law relationship acquired through inter-ethnic marriage.

Another reason for caution is that these data tend to be very broadly interpreted as support for ethnic minority separatism. For instance, separate schooling tends to be a common focal point for those minorities who favour some form of separate development, but these views might be limited only to education policy. It is quite plausible for some minorities to back various 'staying apart' strategies in specific areas (say, schools or marriage) while accepting an open, 'mixing' approach in others (such as toward co-workers or neighbours). Equally, 'staying apart' may be only a feasible, and therefore appealing, option in areas which minorities believe they can influence, or perhaps control (typically marriage partners), as opposed to others where they are predisposed to pragmatism and flexibility (who moves in next door, for instance).

OVERVIEW

As anticipated, the evidence from the electoral data makes it exceedingly difficult to draw generalisations about the structure of public and group opinion on racial and ethnic affairs. Drawing lessons from it for politicians and policy-making is, therefore, not easy. That said, some things can be said with reasonable certainty. First, there appears to be little or no backing at either the aggregate or sub-group level for bold, US-style approaches to public policy on race relations. Specifically, positive discrimination is viewed with deep suspicion, leading some to speculate that the British example is seen as unique and, possibly, founded in different philosophical principles.

Second, it is fair to say that there is little to support the claim that white public opinion acts as a hidden veto on selective reform measures and practices. This is significant because of the widespread assumption made in political life that such a veto both exists and can be rallied with only the mildest stimulation. The notion of equal opportunities is supported by a substantial slice of white opinion, a picture that has more in common with minority opinion than not. Third, preferential treatment is seen as a laudable goal of policy by very different sets of supporters among different ethnic groups. Pakistani and Bangladeshi opinion contains clear elements of support, while Indian and black Caribbean opinion does not. Finally, when it comes to strategies for integrated versus separate development, there is fairly high consistency in opinion across all groups, with the notable exception of Bangladeshis. Three in five among this group report more benefit – to society – from staying apart than mixing together. This, arguably, represents a high degree of potential support for a separatist strategy, in some spheres at least, if not all. Policy-makers should note that this view might also mask a deep reservoir of alienation based on poor conditions, scarce opportunities and on-going immigrant transition difficulties.

6. CANDIDATES AND REPRESENTATION

A decade ago the first wave of ethnic minority MPs in modern times were elected to the House of Commons. Many believed that a new era in ethnic minority representation had begun. The 1987 intake of four minority MPs was augmented by a further two in the 1992 election, as well as by a short-lived by-election victor in late 1991. By the 1997 election campaign, the underlying expectation was that a further increase in the elected tally was possible. Two questions lay behind the headline story of continuing advancement. First, had minority candidates, who are often viewed with suspicion by selectors, proved to be electoral liabilities? The tacit belief over the years has been that parties are rational choice actors, risk-averse in shunning ethnic minorities as potential candidates. This view, however, was based on very limited, and probably distorting, evidence. Second, was it the ethnicity of ethnic minority candidates that mattered above all else to voters generally and to specific sets of voters? The traditional pattern of minority candidates seeking election in areas of high minority concentration had naturally reinforced the perception that such nominees could prove useful in mobilising the minority electorate. This, in turn, led some to argue that this pattern had turned into a mould, and one that served to constrain long term ethnic minority political ambitions.

CANDIDATE FORTUNES IN 1997

In the 1997 general election the total volume of minority candidates standing for mainstream parties reached an all-time high (44), up substantially from the figure in 1992 (24). At the election itself, a record nine hopefuls were returned. As Table 16 shows, all the successful candidates wore Labour's colours, and the only Tory minority incumbent went down to a clear and predictable defeat.

ASSETS AND LIABILITIES

The problem for many of the minority candidates in 1997 was that, as in previous elections, they faced hopeless seats. The seemingly high strike-rate of nine elected out of 44 candidacies tends to mask the fact that two-thirds stood no chance of being elected. Raw totals of candidates selected, while encouraging, can therefore be misleading. As recently as 1992, the total number of candidacies was just 24, compared with only five in 1979. Party label, too, does not automatically signify progress for minority representation. For instance, in 1997 Labour fielded just 13 minority candidates, only a handful more than their Tory rivals. However, the vast majority of Labour's candidates were successfully elected, and it was comparatively rare to observe Labour minorities facing dismal prospects. In contrast, the picture facing nearly all the Tory candidates was extremely poor, even before allowing for the heavy rout experienced by the party nationally. The Liberal Democrats, meanwhile, outstripped both their rivals, with no real prospect of any candidate being elected, though Kerr in south London achieved the only positive swing from among all 17 hopefuls.

It is always difficult to establish whether ethnic minority candidates faced any special penalty because of their ethnic background. Previous tests along these lines have produced unclear evidence and ambiguous conclusions.[29] Taken together in relation to their party's national fortunes, it is possible to isolate some patterns. Conservative minority candidates experienced a smaller than average decline in their share of the vote (-9.3 per cent compared with -11.2 per cent). In two cases, Choudhury in Bethnal Green and Bow and Riaz in Bradford West, spectacular pro-Tory swings were achieved, significantly out of line with the party's performance anywhere else in the country.

Table 16. Ethnic minority parliamentary candidates (main parties), 1997

Candidate and change in party's share of vote (names in bold elected in 1997)	Constituency	1992 result & majority	1997 result & majority	1992-97 swing
LABOUR CANDIDATES (14)				
D. Abbott* +6.4	Hackney North & Stoke Newington	Lab / 30.9	Lab / 47.6	8.3
P. Boateng* +15.4	Brent South	Lab / 26.5	Lab / 57.1	15.3
B. Grant* +13.2	Tottenham	Lab / 26.7	Lab / 53.6	13.4
R. Hoyle +7.7	Hampshire East	Con / 33.1	Con / 19.4	6.6a
P. Khabra* +14.7	Ealing Southall	Lab / 9.0	Lab / 39.2	15.1
Q. Khan +2.3	Aberdeenshire West & Kincardine	Con / 10.5	LD / 6.2	8.3a
O. King** -7.2	Bethnal Green & Bow	Lab / 27.7	Lab / 25.3	5.9
A. Kumar** +11.4	Middlesbrough South & Cleveland East	Con / 2.4	Lab / 19.8	11.1
J. Lehal +12.6	Bedfordshire North East	Con / 39.4	Con / 11.7	13.8
C. Mannan# -5.2	Christchurch	Con / 40.4	Con / 3.6	18.3a
M. Sarwar** +1.1	Glasgow Govan	Lab / 15.4	Lab / 9.0	2.4b

Candidate and change in party's share of vote (names in bold elected in 1997)	Constituency	1992 result & majority	1997 result & majority	1992-97 swing
A. Sayed + 2.1	Argyll & Bute	LD / 7.2	LD / 17.0	2.9b
M. Singh** - 11.7	Bradford West	Lab / 19.4	Lab / 8.5	5.5
K. Vaz* + 9.0	Leicester East	Lab / 22.8	Lab / 65.5	9.4

CONSERVATIVE CANDIDATES (11)

J. Arain - 15.7	Derby South	Lab / 7.4	Lab / 31.1	11.9
K. Choudhury + 4.7	Bethnal Green & Bow	Lab / 27.7	Lab / 25.3	5.9c
N. Deva*** - 13.7	Brentford & Isleworth	Con / 2.8	Lab / 25.7	14.3
B. Khanbai - 14.5	Norwich South	Lab / 7.8	Lab / 28.0	10.1
M. Kotecha - 6.2	Liverpool Walton	Lab / 59.9	Lab / 67.3	3.4d
M. Riaz - 0.8	Bradford West	Lab / 19.4	Lab / 8.5	5.5
A. Scantleberry - 14.1	Tottenham	Lab / 26.7	Lab / 53.6	13.4
G. Sidhu - 12.9	Blackburn	Lab / 11.0	Lab / 30.4	9.7
R. Skinner - 6.6	Bradford North	Lab / 15.7	Lab / 30.5	7.4

Candidate and change in party's share of vote (names in bold elected in 1997)	Constituency	1992 result & majority	1997 result & majority	1992-97 swing
S. Vara - 7.1	Birmingham Ladywood	Lab / 50.1	Lab / 60.8	4.9
N. Zahawi - 11.4	Erith & Thamesmead	Lab / 11.4	Lab / 41.9	15.3

LIBERAL DEMOCRAT CANDIDATES (19)

C. Anglin - 5.5	Leyton & Wanstead	Lab / 14.9	Lab / 38.6	11.9
K. Appiah - 2.8	Lewisham Deptford	Lab / 33.0	Lab / 56.1	11.6
A. de Freitas + 5.4	Great Grimsby	Lab / 14.8	Lab / 37.7	11.5
A. de Souza - 6.3	Crawley	Con / 3.7	Lab / 23.2	13.4
A. Gupta - 4.0	Ealing North	Con / 15.6	Lab / 12.4	14.0
S. Islam - 13.8	Bethnal Green & Bow	Lab / 27.7	Lab / 25.3	5.9c
K. Kerr + 1.6	Vauxhall	Lab / 29.5	Lab / 47.8	3.1d
A. Khan - 4.2	Ilford South	Con / 4.8	Lab / 28.4	f
K. Lee - 1.6	Rutland & Melton	Con / 40.1	Con / 16.8	14.5
R. Martins - 3.3	Hornchurch	Con / 19.0	Lab / 12.9	16.0

Candidate and change in party's share of vote (names in bold elected in 1997)	Constituency	1992 result & majority	1997 result & majority	1992-97 swing
S. Marwa - 0.2	Birmingham Ladywood	Lab / 50.1	Lab / 60.8	4.9
J. Motabudul - 1.1	Leicester East	Lab / 22.8	Lab / 65.5	9.4
P. Munisamy - 7.2	Gloucester	Con / 8.7	Lab / 14.3	11.5
P. Nandra - 4.7	Harrow West	Con / 32.7	Lab / 2.4	17.5
A. Qadar - 1.7	Sheffield Central	Lab / 40.7	Lab / 46.4	2.9d
G. Saluja - 0.2	Dundee East	Lab / 12.3	Lab / 24.6	6.2e
B. Sharma - 2.6	Harrow East	Con / 19.1	Lab / 17.1	18.1
E. Waller - 0.8	Halifax	Lab / 0.8	Lab / 22.2	10.7
Y. Zalzala - 0.6	Manchester Withington	Lab / 21.4	Lab / 42.2	10.4

*   Re-elected incumbent
**   Newly elected
*** Defeated incumbent
# Figures given for 1992 general election (subsequent by-election in 1992-97 parliament)

All swings shown are Conservative to Labour, unless indicated as follows:
a Conservative to Liberal Democrat   b Labour to Scottish National Party
c Labour to Conservative   d Liberal Democrat to Labour
e Scottish National Party to Labour   f swing calculation not possible

Sources: Author's calculations based on: 'Election Results 1997', *The Times*, 3 May 1997; 'British Parliamentary Constituencies 1992-97' (data set compiled by P. Norris); and P. Norris, *UK Election Results [New Constituency Boundaries]*, Cambridge, Mass: Harvard University, 1996

In comparison, Labour's minority candidates did rather poorly, experiencing a smaller than average rise in their share of the vote. (+5.1 per cent against +9.1 per cent nationally). This was chiefly caused by under-performance among many of the candidates in no-hope seats, often squeezed out by tactical surges for Liberal Democrats seeking to unseat Tories.

Oddly, quite the opposite effect was seen with the substantial positive swings experienced by several incumbents, mostly, though not wholly, standing in inner London seats (ranging from +8 to +15 per cent). In these cases it is now reasonable to claim that, far from experiencing an ethnic penalty, there is evidence of an ethnic dividend at work. Many of these MPs had experienced damaging falls in their share of the vote when first returned to Parliament in previous elections. Some had been caught at the short end of continuing local haemorrhaging of the Labour vote in the 1980s. Others had fallen victim to voter-hostility to Labour in quarrels over candidate selection. However, by 1997 several of these minority politicians had developed strong local reputations as constituency MPs and thus benefited from a personal vote. Old arguments portraying minorities as political liabilities suddenly appeared hollow.

CANDIDATE SELECTION ROWS

The other feature of ethnic minority representation in recent years has been the degree to which the question has been associated with controversy and discord. The mid 1990s were especially characterised by rows over so-called 'ethnic entryism' in Constituency Labour Parties serving sizeable minority populations, and where expectations had risen for the election of minority representatives. Furthermore, these disputes often included allegations of corruption, vote-rigging and even intimidation. Cases such as Birmingham Sparkbrook and Small Heath, Manchester Gorton and Glasgow Govan stood out in particular. For the most part these arguments were limited to Labour circles and had the effect of increasing pressure on the party to be seen to be adopting larger numbers of minority candidates in winnable seats. In some cases, such as Bethnal Green and Bow, this was with the consequence of – critics might say at the price of – all three main parties fielding minority candidates, a scenario described locally as 'music to the ears' of the far-right British National Party.

The Conservatives were not entirely immune from these arguments either. The 1992 election had seen to that with the bitter after-taste of John Taylor's failed bid to become the Tory MP for the winnable seat of Cheltenham. This episode had left two stains. First, it was evident that the early status and position of any minority Conservative MP was always likely to be weak and vulnerable. The one term, slightly lacklustre tenure of Nirj Deva in Brentford between 1992-97 highlighted this fragility. Second, the party plainly contained many activists who felt deeply uncomfortable with the idea of an ethnic minority MP. Taylor's experience merely served to bring into the open these dilemmas, though he complained with some justification that he had been let down by a Central Office leadership that was wedded only to the symbolic value of his candidacy and not to its substantive content.[30]

One of the main forces behind these rows had been the implicit equation between minority representatives on the one hand and geographic minority concentrations on the other. Many within the major parties had grown accustomed to the notion of a 'minority constituency', to the extent that they viewed such seats as more hopeful, perhaps more legitimate, territory for ambitious ethnic minority political elites. The evidence itself pointed in this direction, with almost all successful ethnic minority candidates being selected and then elected in 'suitable' seats. Those who were not were often seen as fish out of water.

The sole and significant exception was Ashok Kumar, elected for Middlesbrough South and Cleveland East, where just 0.4 per cent of his constituents belong to an ethnic minority group. Kumar, of course, had previously won a by-election shortly before the 1992 election in a predecessor seat, though he had lost it at the subsequent general election. His fresh success in 1997 therefore amounted to more than a rogue, one-off example. For one thing, it signalled that a future existed for minority representatives beyond the typical seats that had hitherto accommodated their ambitions. For another, in securing an impressive 11.1 per cent swing, he demonstrated that his performance was, if anything, ahead of the curve for most successful minority candidates. This time there was no question of ethnic penalties, and he was viewed as an electoral asset both locally and nationally. Finally, his experience signalled a number of important questions about the longer-term political integration of ethnic minorities in British representative democracy. Certainly, his success was not obtained at the price of racial invisibility, and his appeal in terms of Labour's mainstream campaign was difficult to mistake. Those looking ahead at ethnic minority political representation and participation in ten, perhaps twenty, years from now might reasonably suggest that Kumar's example could be the beginning of an important trend.

OVERVIEW

It would be naive to pretend that the old doubts about ethnic minority candidates in mainstream electoral politics have disappeared. Arguably, they have not, and a current generation of minority political elites is faced with hard, and often insoluble, dilemmas in furthering their political careers in a white-dominated political environment. That said, the 1997 general election results are important because of the powerful rebuttal served to the candidate-liability thesis, at least among several pre-established ethnic minority MPs. After the 1997 election it is that much harder for selectors to resist such candidacies, though not impossible. The other powerful lesson from these results has been the genuinely path-breaking achievements of Kumar in the north east. As a consequence of this breakthrough, the long-term risk of even successful minority candidates being 'trapped' in specific types of seats will probably diminish to a small but significant degree.

Talk of possible breakthroughs aside, serious doubts persist about the openness and fairness of the parties' candidate selection systems and practices. The rows and disputes mentioned previously are perhaps emerging as a symptom of underlying unease about the evenness of the playing field as a whole. For this central reason, it is expected that parties will come under greater pressure to address their internal recruitment mechanisms in a transparent and accountable manner. As part of this process, there are legitimate expectations that all the parties will show willingness in adopting new and innovative mechanisms to promote ethnic minority participation as activists and officials, and not merely as candidates. Adoption of more transparent and objective candidate specification criteria in these procedures is one obvious starting point to extend minority involvement and to tackle some of the sources of recent tension.

7. CONCLUDING REMARKS

This report has been concerned with change and continuity in the political participation of Britain's black and Asian ethnic minorities. It has shown that several unmistakable patterns from earlier elections still persist. Some of these, such as the Labour Party's massive command of the votes of minority electors, cannot be dismissed easily. The real challenge, though, is to account for the continued poor performance of Labour's rivals. Equally significant is the fact that many of the social and economic divisions found within the white electorate are also present among minority voters, but that they are not generally associated with profound differences in electoral behaviour. Politics, it seems, is the chief exception to the wider picture of social and economic integration for Britain's ethnic minorities.

Plainly, ethnic minorities are still a long way from 'fitting' any of the 'conventional' assumptions and parameters about the British electorate. This report suggests that it might be more useful to ask why they should 'fit' such an assumption, because the tendencies towards greater volatility in the electorate as a whole may be delayed rather than absent in the case of minority voters. Despite many superficial contrasts with their white counterparts, arguably the most important feature of the minority electorate has been the degree of party loyalty it has demonstrated over the past quarter of a century. Ironically, this has been an especially dismal era for Labour's broader electoral record. The loyalty to Labour shown by minorities generally has therefore mattered, in the sense that this group's contribution has made the difference between electoral defeat and electoral oblivion. As such, it is a pretty large debt. Whether, and how far, party activists and others attempt to play on this point is a vexed issue. In the short run, the problems for those who wish to gather political spoils for this debt are essentially twofold. First, Labour's large margin of victory in 1997 served, if anything, to dilute the contributions of minority supporters. With most minorities already 'in the bag', Labour turned its gaze to uncommitted white voters in 1997 (mainly by concentrating on marginal seats where minorities are less densely located) and prospered as a consequence. Second, Labour, unlike its rivals, has unambiguously signalled its unwillingness to adopt, let alone implement, racially explicit public policy pledges. If minority supporters are to receive political spoils, this will have to be via an indirect mechanism that targets social, economic, generational and geographic groups – and not ethnic groups.

Cross-party interest in ethnic minority voters is likely to grow considerably at the next general election, precisely because it is thought unlikely that Labour will win such an overwhelming victory. The contributory weight of minorities for Labour will therefore expand under these circumstances, as will the significance of this group of voters in the eyes of Conservative and Liberal Democrat strategists. The politics of the 'ethnic vote' is set to grow in prominence for these reasons, and will be a process that will no doubt accelerate sharply on the back of genuine minority voter drift from Labour to its rivals. To date, this evidence has been fairly sketchy, though the report has shown some clear headway being made by these competitors among sections of the minority electorate. Whether and how far mid-term unpopularity for a Labour administration fuels this process is hard to gauge at present.

The report has also uncovered important variations within the minority electorate, both in terms of its involvement patterns as well as its electoral loyalties. There is little point at present in trying to draw grand generalisations from this picture, since earlier predictions of massive black electoral abstention and Asian rightward defection have amounted to very little. What can be said is that such participation and partisanship issues are really only one part of a bigger picture. The question of electoral geography is a dimension that, despite its superficial appeal, has been poorly understood by activists and commentators alike. By targeting political messages at constituency or local level, parties can do much to fine-tune their appeals to those groups of voters who really matter. Minority voters are not necessarily excluded from this logic, though of course the vast bulk of them reside in constituencies of comparatively modest appeal to the parties. In the past this has amounted to a recipe for the virtual disenfranchisement of many minority voters. Neither hardcore abstention nor strong Labour bias has been the cause. In fact, it is because of the diminished dividends of electoral geography, above all else, that minority political leaders and others have understandably complained of 'falling between the cracks' of the political system.

Two factors are likely to change the dynamics of this reality in the future. The first is fairly obvious, since it relates to fresh patterns of internal migration among minorities from solid Labour strongholds to seats that happen to be more socially and politically mixed in character. This secular trend, in the sense that it is largely unconnected to politics itself, will have major knock-on consequences for the actual places in which minority votes are courted. The second factor is the gradual loosening of political opinion and attitudes among minorities that currently reinforce their political outlook and eventual behaviour. This report has shown that a certain amount of pluralism in opinion and attitudes is already present. It might even be that a sufficiently large segment of minority voters in fact currently back political parties in spite, not because, of those parties' policy commitments and images. The report has also shown that the relationship between so-called ethnic issues and the mainstream political agenda is not easy to define. Political parties that are sensitive and awake to this complex relationship are also likely to be well placed to take advantage of eventual shifts in political behaviour. To argue that in the late 1990s all minority political attitudes are reducible to simplistic 'race agendas' or indeed to flatline 'colour-blindness' is to stretch credulity. Parties and their leaders must therefore choose to engage this complexity, with its attendant costs and risks, or else ignore it, with potentially even greater cost to the quality of the democratic process. Political strategies that are based on short term aversion to this task, however they are brokered within the parties, are likely to be purchased at a longer term expense. The 1997 general election served as a useful illustration of this dilemma. The precise nature and consequences of this delicate trade-off in the next election remain to be seen.

NOTES AND REFERENCES

1. Britain, of course, has not experienced any large-scale political debate over basic voting rights attached to citizenship. Cf. J. Crowley, 'Paradoxes in the politicisation of race: a comparison of Britain and France', *New Community*, vol.19, no.4, 627-43.

2. Cf. A. Hargreaves and J. Leaman (eds), *Racism, Ethnicity and Politics in Contemporary Europe*, Aldershot: Edward Elgar, 1995.

3. Estimates provided by D. Owen (CRER, Warwick) in *The Runnymede Bulletin* (March 1997), p.5.

4. V. Robinson, 'Boom and gloom: the success and failure of Britain's South Asians', in C. Clarke et al. (eds), *South Asian Communities Overseas*, Cambridge: Cambridge University Press, 1990.

5. By polling day, the age of the 1997 register was 74 days – or rather, less than the 116 days average age of the register in the ten elections since 1964.

6. Cf. 'Black Britain', *British Public Opinion* (MORI, July 1996).

7. Cf. CRE, *Ethnic Minorities and the 1983 General Election*, London: CRE, 1984, p.4; A. Ali and G. Percival, *Race and Representation: ethnic minorities and the 1992 elections*, London: CRE, 1993.

8. M. Le Lohe, 'Participation in elections by Asians in Bradford', in I. Crewe (ed), *The British Political Sociology Yearbook – Volume Two: The Politics of Race*, London: Croom Helm, 1975; M. Le Lohe, 'A study of non-registration among ethnic minorities', University of Bradford working paper, 1987; M. Le Lohe, 'Ethnic minority participation and representation in the British electoral system' in S. Saggar (ed), *Race and British Electoral Politics*, London: UCL Press, 1998.

9. 'The campaign will urge Black people to use their vote', *The Guardian*, 2 December 1996; this story for instance made claim to an OBV suggestion that data in the July 1996 MORI poll 'Black Britain' showed that 86 per cent of Black people between 18-25 did not intend to vote. The director of MORI, Simon Braunholtz, was forced to pen a short newspaper letter pointing out gross manipulation of this poll; see: 'The Black vote', letter to *The Guardian*, 15 January 1997. The role of OBV in this controversy is difficult to disentangle from wider disputes over the use made by the press of this crucial, though misinterpreted, poll.

10. 'Most young blacks will not vote', *The Guardian*, 9 January 1997.

11. Cf. C. Swain, *Black Faces, Black Interests: The Representation of African Americans in Congress*, Cambridge, Mass: Harvard University Press, 1993.

12. See S. Saggar (ed), *Race and British Electoral Politics*, London: UCL Press, 1998, for a recent cross-section of academic analyses of the subject.

13. The first initiative by Conservative Central Office in this area was the establishment in 1976 of a dedicated Department of Community Affairs. The department thereafter created a small Ethnic Minorities Unit, itself the precursor of the party's better known Anglo-Asian and Anglo-West Indian Conservative Societies in the late 1970s. Cf. Z. Layton-Henry, *The Politics of Immigration*, Oxford: Blackwell, 1992.

14. See for instance: 'Major woos Asian voters as campaign goes to Calcutta', *The Times*, 10 January 1997; 'Ethnic vote for Tories so small that party has nothing to lose by chasing it', *The Independent*, 15 January 1997; 'Racism must be tackled: John Major should prove his Euro-credentials' (leader), *The Guardian*, 28 January 1997; 'Tug of war for the Asian vote', *The Express*, 3 March 1997.

15. 'Black Britain', *British Public Opinion* (MORI, July 1996); 'Asian Poll: preliminary results', unpublished briefing notes (MORI, March 1997).

16. 'Slick Hague offers fresh start', *The Guardian*, 17 February 1998. For a fuller discussion of Tory options on this front, see: S. Saggar, 'A late, though not lost, opportunity: ethnic minority electors, party strategy and the Conservative Party', *The Political Quarterly*, vol.69, no.2, 148-59, 1998.

17. Cf. G. Alderman, *The Jewish Community in British Politics*, Oxford: Clarendon Press, 1983.

18. P. Norris, 'Anatomy of a Labour landslide', *Parliamentary Affairs*, 50: 509-32, October 1997.

19. Cf. S. Saggar, 'Pipeline politics', *India Today*, 31 March 1997.

20. 'Asian Poll: preliminary results', MORI, March 1997.

21. For an extended discussion on this point, see: S. Saggar, 'Race and voting: some conceptual and theoretical concerns', in S. Saggar (ed), *Race and British Electoral Politics*, London: UCL Press, 1998.

22. Cf. S. Saggar, 'The dog that did not bark: Immigration and race and the general election', in A. Geddes and J. Tongue (eds), *Labour's Landslide*, Manchester: Manchester University Press, 1997, Table 10.4, p.154.

23. Community Relations Commission, *Participation of Ethnic Minorities in the General Election of October 1974*, London: CRC, 1975.

24. Zee TV commissioned the March 1997 MORI poll of Asian voting intentions.

25. The sole race or immigration theme that appeared in an unrehearsed manner was the intervention of Nicholas Budgen, the Conservative incumbent defending Wolverhampton South

West. Budgen's claim was Powellite in tone, sought to high-light white fears about racial integration in his constituency, and received fairly prominent press coverage. Significantly, the party's national campaign managers also rebutted it and the general issue promptly disappeared from the election agenda.

26. Cf. 'Unhappy anniversary' (leader), *The Times*, 19 June 1998.

27. Cf. M. Banton, *Promoting Racial Harmony*, Cambridge: Cambridge University Press, 1985; I. Crewe, 'Representation and ethnic minorities in Britain', in K. Young and N. Glazer (eds), *Ethnic Pluralism and Public Policy*, London: Heinemann, 1983.

28. A. Geddes, 'Asian and Afro-Caribbean representation in elected local government in England and Wales', *New Community*, vol.20, 43-57; S. Saggar and A. Geddes, 'Positive and negative racialisation: the politics of candidate selection', mimeo, April 1998.

29. M. FitzGerald, 'Are blacks an electoral liability?', *New Society*, 8 December 1983.

30. J. Lovenduski and P. Norris, *Political Recruitment: Gender, race and class in the British Parliament*, Cambridge: Cambridge University Press, 1994.

NOTE ON METHODOLOGY

The research featured in this paper is based on a specially conducted ethnic minority booster sample survey. The project aimed to boost the number of ethnic minority respondents in the main cross-section study in the 1997 British Election Study (BES) to a sufficiently reliable level for generalised analysis. Fieldwork for the BES was carried out immediately after the May 1997 general election by Social and Community Planning Research (SCPR).

A combined data set of 705 cases was achieved, drawn from three main sources:

- ethnic minority respondents generated by the main study (106 cases);

- ethnic minority respondents generated by a large-scale screening exercise in areas of high ethnic minority concentration (405 cases); and

- ethnic minority respondents generated by next-door screening at certain sample points with high ethnic minority concentrations (194 cases).

A series of weighting variables were later added to the data set in order to take account of, first, the differing selection probabilities of respondents from the three sample types, and second, the results of an electoral registration and turnout check based on marked-up electoral registers retained by the Lord Chancellor's Department for one year after the election.

The comparative analysis of the main ethnic groups identified in the study was achieved by the creation of a single (weighted) merged file into which the main cross-section and booster respondents were placed. White respondents were obviously drawn from the former (a total of 2,906 cases, then down-weighted to reflect over-sampling in Scotland), while ethnic minority respondents were drawn from different components of the merged file (705 cases in total, then subject to adjustment through weighting). All relevant tables cited in the paper indicate the merged file as their source (using data released by SCPR in December 1997 and March 1998), though some weighting factors in certain tables remain provisional. In any case, cross-checks on data released later confirmed that no substantial alterations in the study's empirical findings result from further weighting of the data.

Finally, it should be added that the use of a special boost was necessary in order to investigate substantive hypotheses. The original sampling frame of the BES was not expected to deliver a sufficiently large number of ethnic minority respondent cases, although the final merged file made full use of those hundred or so cases. As the bulk of the booster cases were drawn from areas of moderate to high ethnic minority residential concentration, there was a residual concern that this might introduce a bias into the findings. Tests using multi-level modelling, however, indicate that no discernible bias was associated with this sampling strategy, although use of a wider range of sampling points would be encouraged in any follow-up research in this field.

Table S11. Sample profile: moved to Britain (of those not British-born)

	white %	Indian %	Pakist %	Bangla %	Bl-Af %	Bl-Car %	Misc %
Pre 1955	2.6	1.1	.0	.0	4.3	2.4	2.0
55 to 64	11.2	10.8	15.1	10.4	54.8	17.1	19.2
65 to 69	23.5	12.9	11.3	5.2	20.4	24.4	17.5
70 to 74	18.9	20.4	17.0	7.8	10.8	22.0	16.3
75 to 79	19.9	19.4	11.3	6.5	1.1	19.5	13.9
80 to 84	10.2	11.8	17.0	10.4	2.2	2.4	9.2
85 to 97	13.8	23.7	28.3	59.7	6.5	12.2	21.9
Total %	100.0	100.0	100.0	100.0	100.0	100.0	100.0

Source: BES 1997

FURTHER READING

Alderman, Geoffrey. 1983. *The Jewish Community in British Politics.* Oxford: Clarendon Press.

Amin, Kaushika and Robin Richardson. 1992. *Politics for All: Equality, Culture and the General Election 1992.* London: Runnymede Trust.

Anwar, Mohammed. 1996. *Race and Elections.* London: Routledge.

Crewe, Ivor. 1983. 'Representation and ethnic minorities in Britain'. In *Ethnic Pluralism and Public Policy*, ed. Young, Ken and Nathan Glazer. London: Heinemann.

CRC. 1975. *Participation of Ethnic Minorities in the General Election of October 1974.* London: Community Relations Commission.

CRE. 1980. *Votes and Policies: Ethnic Minorities and the General Election 1979.* London: Commission for Racial Equality.

CRE. 1984. *Ethnic Minorities and the 1983 General Election.* London: Commission for Racial Equality.

Gouldbourne, Harry (ed). 1990. *Black Politics in Britain.* Aldershot: Avebury.

Heath, Anthony and John Curtice. 1998. 'New Labour, new voters?' Unpublished paper presented to the annual conference of the Political Studies Association, April 1998.

Layton-Henry, Zig. 1978. 'Race, electoral strategy and the major parties'. *Parliamentary Affairs*, 21: 274-75.

Le Lohe, Mich. 1998. 'Ethnic minority participation and representation in the British electoral system'. In *Race and British Electoral Politics*, ed. Shamit Saggar. London: UCL Press.

Messina, Anthony. 1989. *Race and Party Competition*. Oxford: Clarendon Press.

Messina, Anthony. 1998. 'Ethnic minorities and the British party system in the 1990s and beyond'. In *Race and British Electoral Politics*, ed. Shamit Saggar. London: UCL Press.

Norris, Pippa and Joni Lovenduski. 1995. *Political Recruitment: Gender, Race and Class in the British Parliament*. Cambridge: Cambridge University Press.

Parliamentary Affairs, vol.50, autumn 1998 (special issue on Britain Votes 1997).

Rich, Paul. 1998. 'Ethnic politics and the Conservatives in the post-Thatcher era'. In *Race and British Electoral Politics,* ed. Shamit Saggar. London: UCL Press.

Robinson, Vaughan. 1990. 'Roots of mobility: the social mobility of Britain's black population 1971-87'. *Ethnic and Racial Studies*, 13: 274-86.

Saggar, Shamit. 1997. 'The dog that did not bark: Immigration and race and the general election'. In *Labour's Landslide,*.ed. Geddes, Andrew and John Tongue. Manchester: Manchester University Press.

Saggar, Shamit. 1998a. 'A late, though not lost, opportunity: Ethnic minority electors, party strategy and the Conservative Party'. *The Political Quarterly*, 69:148-59.

Saggar, Shamit. 1998b. 'Smoking guns and magic bullets: The "race card" debate revisited in 1997'. *Immigrants and Minorities*, April 1998.

Saggar, Shamit (ed). 1998c. *Race and British Electoral Politics*. London: UCL Press.

Solomos, John and Les Back. 1995. *Race, Politics and Social Change*. London: Routledge.

Werbner, Pnina and Mohammed Anwar (eds). 1991. *Black and Ethnic Leaderships: The Cultural Dimensions of Political Action*. London: Routledge.

Wieviorka, Michael. 1994. 'Racism in Europe: Unity and Diversity'. In *Racism, Modernity and Identity on the Western Front*, eds. Rattansi, Ali and Sally Westwood. Oxford: Polity Press.